REFLECTIONS OF GREATNESS

REFLECTIONS OF GREATNESS

Ancient Egypt

at The Carnegie Museum

of Natural History

DIANA CRAIG PATCH

THE CARNEGIE MUSEUM OF NATURAL HISTORY

Pittsburgh, Pennsylvania

This publication was made possible through a grant from the
National Endowment for the Humanities, a federal agency.

Published by The Carnegie Museum of Natural History,
Pittsburgh, Pennsylvania 15213

ISBN 0-911239-14-6
LIBRARY OF CONGRESS CATALOG CARD NUMBER 89-62543

Design by Molly Renda.
Photographs by Melinda O. McNaugher.
Line drawings on pages 63 and 98 by Nancy Perkins
and on pages 54 and 81 by Linda A. Witt.
Composition by Marathon Typography Service, Inc.
Printing and binding by Fleetwood Litho and Letter Corporation
with technical assistance by Anthony Brusco.

FRONT COVER: Canopic Jar Lid, ACC. 9007-18.
See also entry 50.

FRONTISPIECE: Relief Depicting Horus as a Falcon.
ACC. 3079-2. See also entry 12.

BACK COVER: Triple Kohl Tube with Monkey,
ACC. 1917-4. See also entry 36.

CONTENTS

No one can undertake a project of this scope without requiring the assistance of a great many people. Any success this catalogue enjoys is due to the hard work and skill of The Carnegie Museum of Natural History staff and the generosity of many colleagues.

I am particularly grateful to Louise Craft, Division of Education, for her editing ability and the care she took in organizing the catalogue's production. Elizabeth Mertz also assisted with this work. The catalogue's well-conceived design is the result of Molly Renda's skills.

The Division of Exhibit Design and Production also aided in this catalogue. The superb photographs are due to the talent and dedication of Melinda O. McNaugher. James R. Senior, Daniel A. Pickering, and Patrick D. Martin built mounts that allow the objects to be displayed to their best advantage, while Nancy Perkins capably undertook two of the line drawings. The other two drawings were rendered by Linda A. Witt, a free-lance artist.

Richard A. Souza, Section of Minerals, assisted in identifying the stones used in many objects, while members of the Sections of Mammals, Vertebrate Fossils, and Birds identified certain animal products and the mummified animals visible in the x-rays.

Since the Egyptian Collection resides in the Division of Anthropology, everyone in that department helped to keep the project moving along in different ways. In particular, Marion Dolan, Teresa A. Hiener, Hazel M. Johnson, Sylvia M. Keller, Jennifer Palmer, and Gloria Ramsey assisted in recording, archival research, and typing. Deborah G. Harding, aided by other members of Anthropology, moved objects to be photographed. The object conservation was admirably handled by Joan S. Gardner, Conservator, with the able assistance of Deborah Casselberry and Tamsen Fuller.

I owe a particular debt to David R. Watters, Associate Curator, Division of Anthropology, who was my Project Co-Director of The Walton Hall of Ancient Egypt, for originally bringing me onto the project and for his confidence in my work throughout the past five years. A special note of gratitude must also go to James B. Richardson, III, Chairman of the Division of Anthropology and Assistant Project Director, for his support and encouragement.

A very special thanks goes to my friends and colleagues in the Department of Egyptian, Classical, and Ancient Middle Eastern Art at The Brooklyn Museum. In particular, I want to acknowledge Richard A. Fazzini, Robert S. Bianchi, Donald Spanel, and Paul O'Rourke for their patience with my many questions and their never-failing willingness to share their expertise with me. Diane Guzman, the Wilbour Librarian, and Mary McKercher, as well as Louise Capuano and Mary Gow, always made me welcome in The Brooklyn Museum and assisted me in many ways.

I owe a particular debt to other colleagues who generously gave of their time answering questions, especially Dieter and Dorothea Arnold, The Metropolitan Museum of Art; Peter Dorman, The Oriental Institute; Brigitte Jaroš-Deckert, Vienna, Austria; Richard Jasnow, Würzburg, West Germany; Peter Lacovara, The Museum of Fine Arts, Boston; Joseph A. Marasco, Jr., Forbes Metropolitan Health Center, Pittsburgh, Pennsylvania; David P. Silverman, The University Museum, The University of Pennsylvania; James Swauger, The Carnegie Museum of Natural History; and Lana Troy, University of Uppsala, Sweden.

Finally, this catalogue would never have been possible without the encouragement and generous assistance of David O'Connor, The University Museum, The University of Pennsylvania, and James F. Romano, The Brooklyn Museum. Although it took a great deal of their time, they read each entry's draft; their comments and suggestions gave me new insights into many objects and Egyptian culture. I will always be grateful for everyone's support, but any errors must remain my responsibility.

FOREWORD

The opening of a major new hall is an exciting event for any museum. Here at The Carnegie Museum of Natural History we have been working toward the completion of The Walton Hall of Ancient Egypt since 1983, when we first received funds from the National Endowment of Humanities to assess our outstanding collection of objects from ancient Egypt and to plan how to exhibit them. We were fortunate at that time to acquire a core of expert consultants who could appraise our artifacts and establish goals for the exhibit. Diana Craig Patch, a Mellon Dissertation Fellow and Ph.D. candidate at The University of Pennsylvania, is one of those who worked with us from the beginning, and her scholarship is evident throughout the new hall. Ms. Patch has had extensive research and teaching experience in Egyptology and she has been responsible, as Project Co-Director of The Walton Hall of Ancient Egypt, for its scholarly content. Other consultants on the project were David O'Connor of The University Museum at The University of Pennsylvania and James F. Romano of The Brooklyn Museum.

In developing the hall, we relied on the expert guidance of knowledgeable staff and of Ms. Patch and the other consultants, who created an anthropological base for the exhibit and interpretative programs. With this approach, the objects in the hall are exhibited as keys to an understanding of the everyday life and society of the ancient Egyptians. The interpretative material in the hall develops many facets of ancient Egypt.

We publish here photographs and descriptions of 175 of the hall's more than 600 objects. (A list of the objects on display but not shown in this catalogue can be found in Appendix 1.) The excellent photographs were made by Melinda McNaugher, staff photographer of The Carnegie Museum of Natural History. The written entries describe the objects, grouped by historical period, in their cultural context.

The National Endowment for the Humanities and the Rachel Mellon Walton Fund of the Pittsburgh Foundation provided crucial financial support for The Walton Hall of Ancient Egypt, which is a project of the Second Century Fund. Many people were responsible for the hall's success. Key museum staff included David R. Watters, Associate Curator of Anthropology, the other Project Co-Director; Joan Gardner, Anthropology Conservator; James Senior, Head of the Division of Exhibit Design and Production and his staff; and Louise Craft, who edited and oversaw production for this book, as well as for our other publications on ancient Egypt. Many other people, too numerous to mention, contributed to the undertaking. This catalogue is a tribute to the efforts of all of them.

The Walton Hall of Ancient Egypt is a reflection of the thorough research of all concerned. It provides the museum visitor with the most reliable and up-to-date information available about each object pictured. For those who cannot visit the exhibit, the catalogue provides an in-depth look at ancient Egypt, its artifacts and culture. For all of us who are intrigued by this remarkable civilization, this catalogue truly presents "reflections of greatness."

James E. King, Director
The Carnegie Museum of Natural History

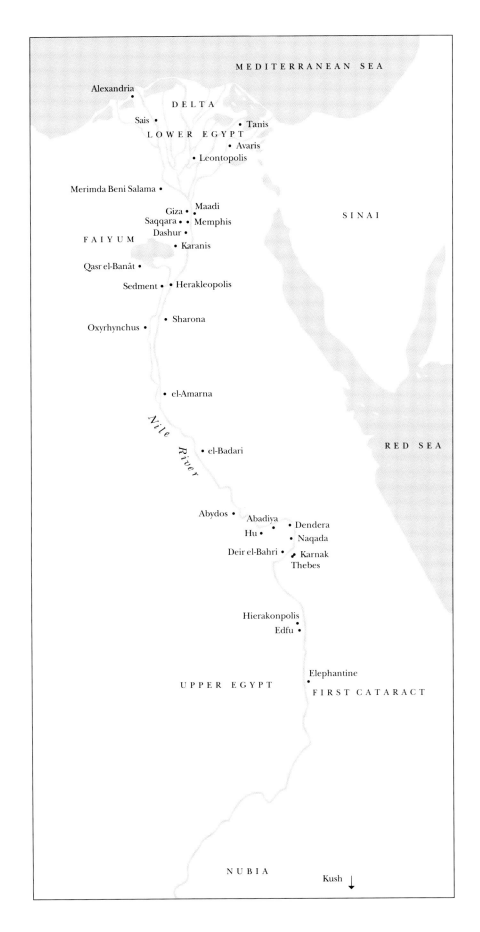

MEDITERRANEAN SEA

Alexandria •

D E L T A

Sais •   • Tanis

L O W E R   E G Y P T

• Avaris

• Leontopolis

Merimda Beni Salama •

Giza • • Maadi

Saqqara • • Memphis

Dashur •

F A I Y U M

• Karanis

Qasr el-Banât •

Sedment • • Herakleopolis

• Sharona

Oxyrhynchus •

• el-Amarna

Nile River

• el-Badari

Abydos •

• Abadiya

• Dendera

Hu •

• Naqada

Deir el-Bahri • ♪ Karnak

Thebes

Hierakonpolis •

Edfu •

Elephantine
•

U P P E R   E G Y P T   F I R S T   C A T A R A C T

S I N A I

R E D   S E A

N U B I A   Kush ↓

S E L E C T E D   A N C I E N T   E G Y P T I A N   S I T E S

PREFACE

In 1896, Andrew Carnegie founded a museum in Pittsburgh, Pennsylvania. The first accession of the new institution was Carnegie's gift of an Egyptian mummy and its coffin, thus establishing the Egyptian collection of The Carnegie Museum of Natural History. Continued local interest in ancient Egypt over the following thirty-five years led to the collection's rapid growth. Today the Egyptian collection at The Museum of Natural History includes almost five thousand objects ranging widely in date and type from Paleolithic stone tools and Predynastic ceramic vessels to Pharaonic funerary equipment and Post-Pharaonic textiles.

The museum acquired the collection through three major sources: The Egypt Exploration Society (EES), purchases, and gifts. Founded in 1882, The Egypt Exploration Society (originally known as The Egypt Exploration Fund) is a London-based association whose purpose remains to this day the systematic excavation of Egyptian archaeological sites. The EES hired professional archaeologists whom the Egyptian Antiquities Organization[1] permitted to excavate and share in the archaeological finds. This division of the excavated objects allowed those museums whose patrons had raised the monetary support necessary for the EES's fieldwork to acquire Egyptian antiquities for their collections. In 1899, Dr. William J. Holland, the director of The Carnegie Museum of Natural History, founded the Pittsburgh Chapter of the EES, which was formally instated in 1901. Between 1899 and 1923, as a result of its financial aid to the EES's archaeological excavations, the museum acquired 1,132 objects.

Nearly seven hundred objects came from the important religious site of Abydos located in Middle Egypt (Accessions 1662, 1917, 2231, 4209, 4210, 4558, 4698, 4918, and 4919). The largest group from this site came from

"middle"-class tombs located in Cemetery D of the North Cemetery; the most important tomb groups from this necropolis, D102, D116, and D119, date through inscriptions to the reigns of Hatshepsut and Tuthmosis III (Accession 1917). Excavations at an area of Abydos called Umm el-Qa'ab, the location of the Early Dynastic royal tombs, led to the acquisition of approximately sixty artifacts belonging to Egypt's first pharaohs (also Accession 1917).

Many Predynastic vessels and some Middle Kingdom funerary goods came from fieldwork at cemeteries at Hu, a site in Upper Egypt (Accessions 1168 and 1234). The EES's excavations at Deir el-Bahri brought to The Carnegie two relief fragments from the Dynasty XI temple there (Accession 3079) and twenty-four votive objects recovered from the Dynasty XVIII temple and its associated chapels built by Pharaoh Hatshepsut (Accession 2940). Smaller investments accorded the museum objects from Egypt's most important ancient city, Memphis (Accession 3755), and Akhenaten's capital city, el-Amarna (Accessions 7043 and 7106). The Ptolemaic and Roman Periods are represented by over one hundred and twenty artifacts from the Faiyum and nearby regions (Accessions 1948, 2231, 2400, 3504, and 4209), including nine fragments of papyri and sixty-seven coins from a large hoard. Among the sites that produced these objects are Batn Harit (Theadelphia), el-Bahnasa (Oxyrhynchus), Hiba, Kom Aushim (Karanis), Qasr el-Banât (Euhemeria), Samahut, Sedment, and Umm el-'Atl (Bacchias).

The collection was further augmented by the purchases of two significant Egyptian collections. The first

---

1. The Egyptian Antiquities Organization of the Egyptian government is in charge of protecting and studying the country's antiquities.

was an assemblage of artifacts collected by Roman Orbeliani on his travels throughout Egypt between 1903 and 1913 (Accession 9074). Four hundred and twenty-six objects included Predynastic pottery, New Kingdom tomb equipment, and Ptolemaic, Roman, and Post-Pharaonic ostraca. The largest part of his assemblage, however, was made up of approximately twenty-three hundred Paleolithic stone tools and specimens of raw Egyptian flint. The second purchase was made in the 1930s from the Münchener Gobelin Manufaktur, a German company that sold The Carnegie a group of nearly five hundred Post-Pharaonic textiles originally collected by the Orientalist F. R. Martin.

The Museum of Natural History obtained the remainder of its Egyptian collection over the years through generous donations of its patrons. In 1901, Andrew Carnegie gave the collection another very important object, a funerary boat of Senwosret III found near the pharaoh's pyramid complex at Dashur. H.J. Heinz and Charles F. Spang both donated portions of their private collections to the museum (Accessions 9007, 21538, 22266, and 29691 and Accession 2983 respectively), and among their pieces were many important Egyptian objects.

One hundred and seventy-five Predynastic and Pharaonic objects from the Egyptian collection are presented in this catalogue, developed in conjunction with the new Walton Hall of Ancient Egypt at The Carnegie Museum of Natural History. Because the collection is in a natural history museum, the Egyptian material is presented from an anthropological perspective. As a result the hall and, therefore, the catalogue interpret ancient Egyptian culture through an examination of the Carnegie objects. The hall is organized around six themes common to many cultures: Cultural Evolution and History, World View, Social Organization, Nautical Tradition, Daily Life, and Funerary Religion; and the objects are used to elucidate each theme. Therefore, the hall and the catalogue emphasize primarily what an object can tell us about ancient Egyptian culture, rather than its place in Egyptian history or its aesthetic value. This unusual focus explains the difference between The Carnegie's exhibit and displays found in traditional art museums.

Approximately one-third of the objects in this catalogue are illustrated independently, occasionally with a close-up photograph or an illustrative drawing. The remainder are shown in group photos since the assemblage is of more interest than any individual artifact. The catalogue is organized chronologically with chapters reflecting the major divisions within Egyptian history, beginning with the Predynastic Period and continuing

through the Roman Period. The dates associated with these periods, the dynastic divisions, and the pharaohs' reigns were developed by integrating recent and well-known chronological studies available for each period.[2] Occasionally in a group photo the range of dates given to the objects extends beyond the time period covered in the chapter.

Although this catalogue is written for the general public, Egyptological information about each piece has been provided for interested scholars. There is a caption for each artifact, although sometimes closely related objects, such as a pair of earrings or a set of canopic jars, are given a single group caption instead of individual ones. Each caption identifies the following:

1. The artifact
2. Its composition (The materials are listed in the order of importance in the object's makeup.)
3. Its date (If the object was excavated, the date reflects that context; otherwise it reflects the most likely chronological range.)
4. Its provenience
5. The most important dimensions (In the case of vessels, these measurements are the object's height and mouth diameter.)
6. Its accession number

Appendix 1 lists the 429 objects in the hall that are not pictured in the catalogue entries. This appendix uses the same caption format as the catalogue entries. Appendix 2 lists the sources where some of our objects have already been published; for the EES material, only the appropriate volume is listed for a general accession number as spatial limitations prevent the individual listing of each object. Appendix 3 is a chronology of ancient Egyptian periods and dynasties. The index includes an abbreviated glossary for people unfamiliar with the specialized terminology used by Egyptologists.

---

2. The following is a list of the sources consulted to develop the chronology, although I remain responsible for any misinterpretations of these works: Fekri Hassan, "Radiocarbon Chronology of Archaic Egypt," *Journal of Near Eastern Studies* 39, no. 3 (1980): 203–07; Fekri Hassan, "Radiocarbon Chronology of Neolithic and Predynastic Sites in Upper Egypt and the Delta," *The African Archaeological Review* 3 (1985): 95–116; K.A. Kitchen, "The Basics of Egyptian Chronology in Relation to the Bronze Age," *High, Middle or Low: Acts of an International Colloquium on Absolute Chronology Held at the University of Gothenburg, 20th–22nd August 1987, Part I*, edited by Paul Astrom, in *Studies in Mediterranean Archaeology and Literatures*, vol. 56 (Gothenburg, Sweden: Paul Astrom Forlag, 1987), pp. 37–55; K.A. Kitchen, *The Third Intermediate Period in Egypt (1100–650 B.C.)* (Warminster, England: Aris & Phillips, 1973); Jurgen von Bekerath, *Handbuch der ägyptischen Königsnamen*, in *Münchener ägyptologishe Studien*, vol. 20 (Munich: Deutscher Kunstverlag, 1984).

Predynastic Period, CIRCA 4500–3100 B.C.

INTRODUCTION

During the Neolithic Period (ca. 5450–4500 B.C.) and the early Predynastic Period (ca. 4500–3850 B.C.), ancient Egypt's inhabitants practiced some agriculture and herded animals, while supplementing their diet with fishing and hunting. These people lived in huts, made pottery and stone tools, had communal granaries, and established cemeteries. Sites illustrating these activities are known from the Faiyum, the Delta (Lower Egypt), and Upper Egypt. Although these different regions practiced the same subsistence patterns, the cultural manifestations of these activities were diverse, resulting in the identification of separate cultural traditions. Within Lower Egypt, for example, the sites of Merimda Beni Salama and Maadi possessed cultural characteristics distinct from contemporary Badarian and Naqada I cultures of Upper Egypt.

The Predynastic Period, the era prior to Pharaonic Egypt, is best known, however, from archaeological evidence recovered at numerous sites, almost exclusively cemeteries, in Upper Egypt. Archaeologists have principally used changes in ceramic styles and wares to divide the Predynastic Period in this region into four phases: Badarian (ca. 4500–3800 B.C.), Naqada I (or Amratian, ca. 3850–3650 B.C.), Naqada II (or Gerzean, ca. 3650–3300 B.C.), and, finally, Naqada III (or Semainian, ca. 3300–3100 B.C.). Although Egyptologists can associate artifacts with each phase, the implications of these objects continue to be explored.

Naqada I sites have been found between Abydos and Hierakonpolis. Their inhabitants practiced agriculture and pastoralism, but also fished and fowled. Living in small scattered villages, still in huts, all individuals appear to have been generally socially equal. The Naqada I culture is identified by skillfully made flint tools, ground stone objects, and certain ceramic wares, especially Black-topped Red Ware vessels. Several large cemeteries, with graves containing everyday equipment as well as figurines and amulets, have provided much information.

During Naqada II, people came to depend heavily on their crops and animals for food. Many new cultural developments, such as metallurgy, irrigation, and large-scale craft production, are revealed in the artifacts from both Naqada II and Naqada III. During both periods, villages and growing towns shared a similar material culture from the Delta to the First Cataract. Boats facilitated communication and the distribution of goods. Artifacts reflecting contact with Syro-Palestine and even Mesopotamia are also known.

During late Naqada II and Naqada III, certain individuals, most likely men, began acquiring power, first within their villages and then probably over regions. Egyptologists believe certain very large tombs containing many funerary goods belonged to these individuals. The cause of this cultural change is uncertain, but perhaps the need to stabilize fluctuations in agricultural production resulting from inconsistent Nile floods led to increased communication and exchange first between villages and subsequently between regions. Successful local leaders of villages that perhaps possessed a recognized cult, a special natural resource, large populations, or agricultural prosperity may have possessed the advantage necessary to expand control over entire districts. The details of Egypt's unification are unclear, but the process must have taken many years. Eventually the districts were united under one ruler, possibly as early as Narmer, but certainly by the reign of 'Aha (ca. 3100 B.C.), the first king of Dynasty I.

1 a-e: Left to right

2 a-e: Clockwise from top left, then center

1.

Predynastic Vessels

(pottery)

a. Red Polished Ware Bowl
Naqada I (ca. 3850–3650 B.C.)
Hu, U225
Height 6 cm; diameter 15 cm
ACC. 1168-50

b. Red Polished Ware Jar
Early Naqada II (ca. 3650–
   3450 B.C.)
Provenience unknown
Height 24.2 cm; diameter 6 cm
ACC. 9074-2309

c. Black-topped Red Ware Jar
Naqada II (ca. 3650–3300 B.C.)
Abydos, E323
Height 34.5 cm; diameter 14 cm
ACC. 4210-14

d. Black-topped Red Ware Bowl
Naqada I (ca. 3850–3650 B.C.)
Hu, U260
Height 8 cm; diameter 10.5 cm
ACC. 1168-90

e. Rough Ware Jar with an
   Internal Strainer
Naqada III (ca. 3300–3100 B.C.)
Hu?
Height 23 cm; diameter 9 cm
ACC. 21537-42

The Predynastic people used a variety of materials to construct containers. Although plant fibers, skins, and occasionally stone were always used, once pottery was invented, baked clay rapidly became the most popular material. Clay's versatility allowed people to experiment with shape and decoration. A clay vessel that was polished or lined with pitch could be made relatively waterproof and, with a lid and seal, airtight. The archaeological record of the Predynastic Period exhibits an abundant variety of ceramic styles. The most popular clay was a Nile Valley silt. One example of this clay is a dark red, highly polished ware that archaeologists call Red Polished Ware (figures 1a and b).

The distinctive black tops on figures 1c and d are a variation of the Red Polished Ware. These Black-topped Red Ware vessels were made by inverting them before they were fired and burying their rims and upper bodies under organic debris while leaving the rest exposed in the kiln. After firing, the top of each vessel was black while the uncovered area remained a dark red, the color of the burnished slip covering the clay body.

Pottery was used on a daily basis to cook, serve, and store food and water. It is likely that the Rough Ware vessel (figure 1e) once held liquids because its neck possesses an internal strainer that allows liquid in and out, but prevents most pieces of dirt from entering. In a sandy country like Egypt, this is important. The restricted neck and thorough polishing on figure 1b suggest that it too contained a liquid. The large Black-topped Red Ware jar (figure 1c) might have stored grain.

Most Predynastic ceramics have been recovered from graves, indicating that in addition to daily use, vessels were buried as grave goods. The lack of indications of wear and the high quality of many of these bowls and jars demonstrate that they were made specifically as burial goods and were not used on a daily basis.

2.

Funerary Goods

a. Small Jar with Lugs
(granodiorite)
Early Naqada II (ca. 3650–
   3450 B.C.)
Abydos, E103
Height 4.3 cm; diameter 4 cm
ACC. 4210-4

b. Diamond-shaped Palette
(slate)
Naqada I (ca. 3850–3650 B.C.)
Abydos, E150
Length 52.6 cm; width 16 cm
ACC. 4210-11

c. Fish-shaped Palette
(slate)
Naqada II (ca. 3650–3300 B.C.)
Naqada/Hu, B21
Length 13.9 cm; height 10.4 cm
ACC. 1948-55

d. Amuletic? Tusk
(ivory, paste)
Late Naqada I–early Naqada II
   (ca. 3750–3500 B.C.)
Provenience unknown
Length 15.4 cm; width 3 cm
ACC. 9074-2660b

e. Comb
(ivory)
Late Naqada I–early Naqada II
   (ca. 3750–3500 B.C.)
Provenience unknown
Length 4.8 cm; width 2.6 cm
ACC. 9074-2660i

When archaeologists find burials containing funerary goods, they assume that the culture under study had developed a belief in an afterlife. The objects placed with the body provided the deceased with equipment necessary for a comfortable life after death. In the afterlife, a per-

3

Eye cosmetics are well known from Pharaonic Egypt. In Predynastic graves, the presence of slate palettes, sometimes with depressions in the stone from use and traces of pigment, is proof that this tradition is old. The diamond shape is a common palette form in the early Predynastic Period (Naqada I, ca. 3850–3650 B.C.). Figure 2b is an unusually large example. Archaeologists accept the idea that graves of individuals who were more important than most people in a community might contain many goods or objects that were larger than average or made from a rare material. These "fancier" graves reflect the wealth and power of these important people, who had access to objects unavailable to others. Therefore, this very large palette may have belonged to an important individual in an era when social stratification was uncommon.

son would need the same items as those used during his or her lifetime. In cemeteries from the Badarian Period (ca. 4500–3800 B.C.), ancient Egyptians were wrapped in linen cloth and buried in their graves with a variety of goods, including pottery vessels, tools made from bone and flint, slate palettes, and jewelry. This began a tradition in Egypt that continued for five thousand years.

At first, ancient Egyptians were probably buried with personal ornaments and items they used on a daily basis, such as tools, vessels, and food. Shortly thereafter, various items were made solely to be used in the afterlife. These objects, for example, the large diamond-shaped slate palette (figure 2b), show no signs of wear.

Not all graves contained the same types or quantities of burial goods. In the Naqada II and III Periods (ca. 3650–3100 B.C.), there was increasing variability among the contents of graves. The most common burial goods throughout the Predynastic Period were ceramic vessels. In addition to the body and its accompanying ceramic vessels, graves generally contained other items: slate palettes for grinding eye paint (figures 2b and c), stone jars (figure 2a), combs (figure 2e), jewelry, knives, projectile points, tools of flint, and, more rarely, figurines, amulets (figure 2d), and copper objects.

3.
Decorated Ware Jar

(pottery, paint)

Naqada II (ca. 3650–3300 B.C.)

Hu, U31

Height 20.5 cm; diameter 12 cm

ACC. 1168-34

This jar is a beautifully made example of a Predynastic ceramic type archaeologists classify as Decorated Ware. Decorated Ware was popular principally in the Naqada II Period (ca. 3650–3300 B.C.) and is identified by decorations in dark red paint on a pale-colored marl clay. Because this clay is restricted to certain desert localities and Decorated Ware illustrates a narrow range of shapes and decorative elements, archaeologists suggest that only a few villages produced this ceramic type, although it was distributed throughout Egypt. This may be our earliest evidence of craft specialization in ancient Egypt.

The decorative schemes on these vessels vary, but water, spirals, desert and riverine animals, boats, and female figures are the most common. This example is decorated with a motif of wavy lines symbolizing water (which later developed into the hieroglyph for water) and triangles representing hills. There are three triangular lugs, two of which are pierced. Since this lug shape is known on earlier vessels from Mesopotamia, archaeologists have suggested that its appearance on Egyptian vessels is one indicator of contact between the two regions, encounters probably based in trade. In a functioning vessel, the holes would have been used to hang the jar from a tripod or other suspension device. Decorated Ware appears, however, to have been funerary pottery and rarely used in settlements.

4.

Jar with a Boat Motif

(pottery, paint)

Naqada II (ca. 3650–3300 B.C.)
Provenience unknown
Height 13 cm; diameter 6 cm
ACC. 14772-4

4

This small jar depicts a Predynastic boat, a familiar motif known from a surprisingly small number of ceramic vessels. These multi-oared boats are consistently represented with one or two small cabins on the deck, often in association with a pole topped by a geometric design. The significance of the poles' iconography has been much disputed, but current scholarship suggests that they are either divine standards or emblems representing districts or towns. Palm(?) fronds like the one on this vessel often decorate the bow. Short wavy lines indicating water are found on the rim and lugs.

Other vessels depict similar boats sometimes in associ-

ation with a female whose upraised arms probably indicate that she is dancing. When she is shown with men, her larger size indicates that she is the most significant individual. These figures suggest that the boats on these jars may represent cult barques instead of traveling boats as has often been assumed. These boat designs are but one piece of evidence identifying growing interest among the early Egyptians in religion and its associated cults. From about the same time, animal and human figurines, symbols later associated with specific Pharaonic gods and goddesses, and a possible temple precinct all hint at developing religious beliefs during the Predynastic Period.

Predynastic Period

5 a-d: Left to right

5.
Wavy-handled Jars

(pottery)

a. Early Naqada II (ca. 3650–
3450 B.C.)
Hu, U46
Height 50.6 cm; diameter
27.3 cm
ACC. 1168-35

b. Naqada III (ca. 3300–
3100 B.C.)
Hu, U397
Height 29.5 cm; diameter 12 cm
ACC. 1168-75

c. Late Naqada III–early
Dynasty I (ca. 3200–3000 B.C.)
Hu, U69
Height 29.5 cm; diameter 9.5 cm
ACC. 1168-38

d. Late Naqada III–early
Dynasty I (ca. 3200–3000 B.C.)
Hu, U47
Height 24.1 cm; diameter 11 cm
ACC. 1168-36

In all man-made objects, fashion and style vary over time. Pottery is one type of material that often reflects gradual change. The short life span of most vessels necessitates constant production, thereby accommodating variation. The four vessels shown here illustrate a gradual evolution of a vessel shape known as Wavy-handled Ware. This style began as a globular jar with ledge-type handles in a wavy pattern (rounder than figure 5a). Slowly over several centuries, the body became a slender cylindrical shape with a rope impression circumscribing the vessel and replacing the wavy handles (figure 5b). After five centuries, the form was a simple short cylinder vessel without markings (figure 5d). The red crosshatch pattern on figure 5c simulates the netting it was once carried in.

The earliest shape, the large round jar with thick wavy handles, is based on a Palestinian form. The Egyptians borrowed this style from that region probably as a result of trade contacts prior to about 3300 B.C. Although Egyptologists know few details concerning early communication between Egypt and Palestine, Egyptian artifacts from the late Predynastic Period (ca. 3300–3100 B.C.) and Dynasty I (ca. 3100–2900 B.C.) have been recovered from the Sinai and southern Palestine. Previously, this contact was believed to be one of military control on the part of the Egyptians, but a better interpretation is trade. The Egyptians probably wanted copper, oils and resins, a source for decent timber that the Nile Valley could not supply, or perhaps even the right-of-way to travel through Palestine to more distant regions where these goods were accessible. What the Palestinians accepted in return is less clear. Perhaps the trade was in perishable goods, such as wheat and barley, which rarely survive in the archaeological record.

Early Dynastic Period, CIRCA 3100–2750 B.C.

Old Kingdom, CIRCA 2750–2250 B.C.

and

First Intermediate Period, CIRCA 2250–2025 B.C.

INTRODUCTION

The Early Dynastic Period (Dynasty I–II, ca. 3100–2750 B.C.) began with 'Aha, whom ancient Egyptian historians recognized as Menes, the first king of a unified Egypt. The foundations of Pharaonic culture, established in the Predynastic Period, were expanded during this time. The king, aided by a government with a growing bureaucracy, controlled Egypt's population and economy. Titles representing administrative positions are documented, with many pertaining to the regulation of agricultural production. Concurrently, writing evolved swiftly from the late Predynastic pictographs to a more complex script, still based on pictures, but capable of recording major events, including military campaigns, heights of Nile floods, founding of temples, and censuses. The founding of ancient Egypt's primary capital, Memphis, occurred at the beginning of Dynasty I.

The king wielded enormous authority and wealth. These resources allowed him to construct the earliest monumental architecture—the royal tombs and cenotaphs—and commission elaborate funerary goods. The king controlled the distribution of goods produced by state-sponsored workshops. Along with new occupations, social classes are now identifiable.

The Old Kingdom (Dynasty III–VI, ca. 2750–2250 B.C.) followed the Early Dynastic Period. The centralized government rapidly developed a complex bureaucracy headed by a powerful, divine king. This bureaucracy assessed and then collected the resources that the king used to further his goals. By Dynasty IV, the kings, still linked to the gods Horus and Seth, intensified their divinity by incorporating the name of the sun god, Re, into their prenomens (names). Soon they were regularly entitled "son of Re" as well. At the capital, Memphis, the king was surrounded by his family and a small group of

nobles who composed the government while the remainder of Egypt's population served him as farmers or craftsmen.

In Dynasty III–IV, princes filled the most important administrative posts. During Dynasty V–VI, competition between the king and the princes encouraged rulers to appoint nonroyal nobles to these positions, a practice that continued for another fifteen hundred years. Continued absolute control over labor and goods enabled kings to build the first Egyptian stone monuments, including the unparalleled pyramid complexes at Giza. Trading expeditions collected exotic goods desired for manufacturing temple and funerary equipment.

Pepy II, the last strong ruler of the Old Kingdom, was succeeded by several short-reigned rulers. The subsequent period of decentralized government, the First Intermediate Period (Dynasty VIII–XI, ca. 2250–2025 B.C.), featured the maintenance of traditional Egyptian culture in the provinces. The causes and processes that led to this decentralization and the development of a provincial nobility are not well understood. The appointment of provincial nobles to administrative positions in Dynasty V–VI certainly gave a new group of people access to power and wealth. As the central authority weakened, these nobles acquired the resources that once gave the king much of his power. Low Nile floods, reducing crop yields, may have also played a part in destabilizing the country.

For whatever reason, during Dynasties IX, X, and the first half of XI, various provinces, headed by local nobles, competed with one another for control. The most successful nobles, such as the governors of Herakleopolis and Thebes, offered stability to the local inhabitants through well-managed farmland and armies for defense, while these two regions developed into competitive king-

Early Dynastic Period, Old Kingdom, and First Intermediate Period

doms. The First Intermediate Period ended when the Dynasty XI Theban king Nebhotepre Mentuhotep (II) reunified Egypt by conquering Herakleopolis.

6.

Magic Knife

(hippopotamus ivory)

Dynasty I, reign of Djer (ca. 3050 B.C.)
Abydos, Tomb of Djer
Length 13.6 cm; width 1.7 cm
ACC. 1917-429

While working at Umm el-Qaab, the Early Dynastic royal cemetery at Abydos, Sir Flinders Petrie found this unusual object during the excavation of Pharaoh Djer's tomb. Made from a hippopotamus tusk that was cut to a thickness of four millimeters, the object has a curved shape and pointed end reminiscent of the magic knives known from the Middle Kingdom (ca. 2025–1627/1606 B.C.). These knives are flat pieces of curved ivory in several styles; often they have an end that tapers to a rounded point. If this identification is right, the Carnegie piece is the earliest-known example of a complete magic knife.

The Main Deposit at Hierakonpolis also produced several objects that may be early knives, although a secure date for this material has not been established.[1] None of the Hierakonpolis artifacts, however, is complete, and several have shapes and decorations that share more attributes with the older, elaborate Predynastic knives than later ones. At one time, the Carnegie knife's pointed end was probably painted to represent the head of a leopard or a snake, decorative elements known on other knives.

In the Middle Kingdom, magic knives often featured representations of protective deities and hieroglyphs for words such as "protection"; sometimes they were inscribed with a complete prophylactic message. Placed under or near beds, these pieces possibly magically warded off snakes, scorpions, and other nighttime dangers. In some cases, the pointed ends are worn, suggesting that they were used to etch circles in the dirt around beds. Sleepers would then be protected because negative forces could not cross these lines. The ancient Egyptians chose hippopotamus ivory because they hoped that the animal's aggressive and dangerous nature would be transferred to these amuletic devices.

1. Barbara Adams, *Ancient Hierakonpolis* (Warminster, England: Aris & Phillips Ltd, 1974), pp. 60–61, 71. Adams calls these objects "wands," also a commonly accepted term.

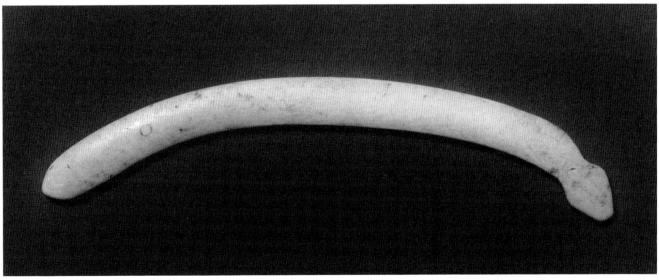

6

7.

Stela Belonging to a Woman

(limestone)

Dynasty I, reign of Den (ca. 3000 B.C.)
Abydos, Tomb of Den
Height 15.6 cm; width 13 cm
ACC. 1917-90

The earliest Egyptian pharaohs built their tombs in an isolated stretch of low desert southwest of the Khentiamentiu temple of Abydos. Two factors may have influenced their choice of Abydos as the royal necropolis. By about 3000 B.C., Abydos already possessed a sacred identity that would intensify with time. Secondly, historical records suggest that the family home of these first kings was This, a city ten kilometers north of Abydos. At least twelve rulers are buried at Abydos and one tomb belongs to Den, the fifth ruler of Dynasty I. His tomb was larger than his predecessors' and records suggest he was one of the most prosperous rulers of this period. Approximately 136 subsidiary graves of retainers surrounded the central chamber of Den's tomb. The concept of a royal tomb surrounded by members of the royal family and loyal officials grew in popularity so that in Dynasty IV-VI (ca. 2675–2250 B.C.) large secondary cemeteries developed around the royal pyramids.

Sir Flinders Petrie discovered this small stela of a female contemporary of Pharaoh Den of Dynasty I. It marked the burial of a woman who bore the titles "She Who Provides [for] Horus" and "She Who Strikes Khesti [Seth]" (ḥtm[.t] ḥr sqr[?].t ḫ3sti).[1] The grave was one of those found around Den's tomb and probably belonged to a member of the royal harem since the titles on this stela correspond to the titulary associated with royal women in Dynasty III-IV (ca. 2750–2565 B.C.). The reference in these titles to Horus and Seth, gods associated with the early pharaohs, may have united the women with the king himself or his position. It is also possible that these titles tied the women to cultic roles. Alternatively, the interpretation may be more simple: They were signs of royal favor. Although this stela's titles are readable, most of this woman's name was intentionally damaged at some point in the past. The feminine t ending and the head of the female determinative glyph, both part of her name, are still visible.

---

1. Assistance in the translation and interpretation of the titles on this stela was graciously given to me by Dr. Lana Troy, Research Assistant, Institute of Egyptology, Uppsala University, Sweden.

Because of typesetting considerations, I have chosen not to capitalize proper nouns in the transliterations.

Early Dynastic Period, Old Kingdom, and First Intermediate Period

8.

Fragment of an Inscribed Bowl

(steatite)

Dynasty I, reign of Qa'a (ca. 2900 B.C.)
Abydos, Tomb of Qa'a
Length 6 cm; width 5 cm
ACC. 1917-338

The early royal tombs contained hundreds of artifacts including many stone vessels buried in secondary chambers. This bowl fragment once was part of such a vessel. Often the grave goods were inscribed or labeled with the pharaoh's name and titles and sometimes with information about festivals, buildings, or shines. This piece clearly bears the name of the Pharaoh Qa'a in the lower left. Above the name, a cobra (left) symbolizing Lower Egypt and a vulture (right) representing Upper Egypt sit above baskets. The cobra and vulture are called the "Two Ladies" and compose a royal title signifying the pharaoh's unification of Egypt's two regions. Visible above the Two Ladies are hieroglyphs belonging to a second royal title, "King of Upper and Lower Egypt." The Two Ladies and the King of Upper and Lower Egypt continued to be primary royal titles throughout Egyptian history, emphasizing the stability of titulary and kingship itself. By about 3000 B.C., other traditional attributes of kingship, such as the Red and White Crowns, the smiting scene, the *heb-sed* festival,[1] and the king represented as a bull, lion, or falcon, were well established.

Artifacts like this inscribed piece from these early royal tombs give Egyptologists the opportunity to study the de-

velopment of hieroglyphs, the earliest written form of the ancient Egyptian language. Objects dating to the end of the Predynastic Period, such as the famous Narmer palette, provide us with the earliest hieroglyphic inscriptions. During the Early Dynastic Period these inscriptions increased in frequency, clarity, and complexity.

---

1. Smiting scenes depict the king about to strike an enemy with a mace or club. This scene, often seen on temple walls, symbolized the king's ability to defend Egypt from its enemies. The *heb-sed* festival was a jubilee that celebrated the rejuvenation of the king's power.

9.

Funerary Goods of Kha'sekhemwy

Dynasty II, reign of Kha'sekhemwy (ca. 2750 B.C.)
Abydos, Tomb of Kha'sekhemwy

---

a. Small Jar
(indurated limestone)
Height 6.3 cm; diameter 2 cm
ACC. 1917-384

b. Bowl
(copper)
Height 8 cm; width 20.3 cm
ACC. 1917-447

c. Deep Bowl
(syenite)
Height 11 cm; diameter 17 cm
ACC. 1917-389

During 1899 and 1900, Sir Flinders Petrie excavated the early royal tombs at Abydos. Kha'sekhemwy, the last pharaoh of Dynasty II (ca. 2750 B.C.), was the final king to build his tomb there. The substructure of his large mastaba contained a central chamber surrounded by fifty-eight compartments. These small storerooms contained items deemed necessary by the ancient Egyptians for their pharaoh's eternal life. Rooms filled with jars of grain were particularly common. Other rooms contained stone vessels, copper tools, flint knives, and clay sealings that covered the tops of jars. These sealings are stamped with the name of the king or one of his officials and are one method archaeologists use to identify the owners of the Abydos tombs.

In one corridor, Petrie recovered a stash of metal vessels, seven gold-capped jars, and model tools of copper. Figure 9a, one of the seven jars, once had a lid that we know was made from sheet gold simulating a piece of cloth laid over the vessel's mouth and tied down with braided gold wire imitating string or rope. This vessel was manufactured in an unusual way. To make a wider

9a-c: Left to right

10

cavity than the jar's mouth allowed, the artisan drilled from the vessel's bottom, producing in the container's base a hole larger than the opening in the mouth. When finished, the craftsman filled the hole with a flawlessly fitted piece of matching stone. Also, the exquisitely polished surfaces of the syenite bowl attest the ancient stone carvers' skills (figure 9c).

The copper bowl (figure 9b) has a simple oval shape with a depressed center that was probably fashioned by beating sheet copper over a wooden form. When buried, the now-crushed bowl lay next to or was encased in linen. As a result, plainweave linen fragments and pseudomorphs (here cloth totally replaced by minerals) remain attached to the bowl's outer edges. In addition, wood impressions, possibly from a nearby box, are found on the bowl's exterior.

10.

Statuette of a Baboon

(faience)

Early Dynastic Period (ca. 3100–2750 B.C.)
Abydos, M220
Height 6.5 cm; width 3.1 cm; depth 3.8 cm
ACC. 2400-7a

Modeled in an early type of faience, this statuette represents an adult male baboon in a seated position. The animal's hands rest on its knees, which are drawn up under the chin. Its genitalia are clearly defined between its legs.

Early Dynastic Period, Old Kingdom, and First Intermediate Period

The baboon had many roles in Egyptian religion. This species rises with the sun and warms up by sitting in the early morning rays; during this time, these baboons tend to socialize. This behavior caused the Egyptians to link this animal to their sun god, Re. The baboon was also an important manifestation of the god of time and recording, Thoth. In ancient Egypt, the male baboon, like all primates, was an erotic symbol and its sexual potency was linked with rebirth. The cycle of birth, death, and rebirth was the most basic religious belief in ancient Egypt.

Many votive statuettes of this type were recovered during excavations in the temple at Abydos dedicated to a jackal god, Khentiamentiu. As was the custom, pious Egyptians probably offered these statuettes to Khentiamentiu in exchange for "his ear," that is, so that he would listen to a personal request. Although this statuette was found in rubbish layers that cannot be solidly dated, its style allows archaeologists to place it in the Early Dynastic Period. Votive objects were kept in temple storerooms. Eventually these rooms became so crowded that the offerings had to be discarded. The religious nature of these pieces probably prohibited their disposal outside the temple precinct, hence the large numbers found below later Abydos temple deposits.

11.

Headrest

(limestone)

Late Old Kingdom (ca. 2565–2250 B.C.)
Provenience unknown
Height 18 cm; width 16.5 cm; depth 7.5 cm
ACC. 9074-2441

A headrest was the ancient Egyptian version of our pillow. People used wooden ones, often padded with strips of linen for comfort, while sleeping or resting on couches or bed platforms. The curved portion was placed under the neck and the user generally slept on his or her side. Often headrests were inscribed with the owner's name and figures or faces of gods and goddesses who could protect the individual during the especially dangerous night hours. The area reserved for the owner's name on this example was never engraved.

This headrest, made in three parts, was carefully modeled in stone. A resin or gum once held the curved portion, the neck, and the flat base together. Its stone composition and the weak joins between the headrest's elements indicate that it was intended solely for use by the deceased in the afterlife and not on a daily basis during his or her lifetime. Headrests recovered from inside coffins had been laid alongside the mummies. A chapter from the "Coming Forth by Day" ("Book of the Dead") informs us that amulets in the shape of headrests protected the deceased from the loss of his or her head in the afterlife.

11

Middle Kingdom, CIRCA 2025–1627/1606 B.C.

and

Second Intermediate Period, CIRCA 1648–1539 B.C.

INTRODUCTION

Pharaoh Mentuhotep II reunified Egypt, ending the turmoil of the First Intermediate Period (ca. 2250–2025 B.C.). During his reign, a centralized bureaucracy reappeared, new monuments were built, and craft centers were reinstated. Mentuhotep was of Theban origin and elevated Thebes to the religious capital of the Middle Kingdom (Dynasty XI–XIII, ca. 2025–1627/1606 B.C.).

The Dynasty XII kings, mostly called Senwosret or Amenemhet, were overall highly successful. These kings greatly expanded the temple at Karnak, encouraging the rise of Amun, later Amun-Re, as Egypt's principal god. Abydos, by this time associated with Osiris, the god of the underworld, became an important pilgrimage site. The rulers also founded a new capital city, It-tawy, near the Faiyum, a fertile area of great interest to them. During Dynasty XII, the kings thoroughly subjugated Lower Nubia by constructing large fortresses that housed military garrisons. Situated on the Nile, the fortresses allowed the Egyptians to control the river's traffic as well as exploit the local inhabitants for cattle, gold, and exotic goods traded from central Africa.

The Middle Kingdom kings, however, were unable to exclude as many people from participating in the fruits of Egyptian culture as their Old Kingdom predecessors. More members of the nobility had access to special goods and services once reserved for only a favored few. Also, groups of people best categorized as "middle" class are first identifiable during the Middle Kingdom through the large number of private statues, stelae, and ex-votos they commissioned.

Ancient Egyptian cultural tradition and the administrative system continued into Dynasty XIII, although a breakdown in royal succession resulted in a series of ephemeral kings. When Dynasty XIII ended, the Second Intermediate Period (Dynasty XV–XVII, 1648–1539 B.C.), a period that marks the end of a unified Egypt, began.

During Dynasty XIII (1801–1627/1606 B.C.), Egypt was subjected to a large-scale influx of foreigners for the first time in its history. One new, aggressive group, the Hyksos, migrated from Palestine. These people took over the northern cities, established their own dynasty (ca. 1648 B.C.), and appointed Egyptians as client kings in Delta city-states. Simultaneously in Thebes, the fifteen kings of Dynasty XVII (1627/1606–1539 B.C.) maintained Egyptian culture and tradition while holding a portion of Upper Egypt, chiefly between Abydos and Elephantine, against foreign expansion from both the Hyksos in the north and the Kushites in the south. When the Dynasty XIII kings lost control of Lower Nubia to locally settled Egyptians, the Upper Nubian kingdom, Kush, quickly incorporated the region into its empire. During the Second Intermediate Period and for the first time in Egyptian history, internal weakness in Egypt coincided with the political growth and prosperity of foreign states. This resulted in foreign control over much of the country for more than one hundred years. Interestingly, both the Hyksos and Kushite kings incorporated Egyptian tradition into their dynasties while challenging their Theban adversary.

Toward the end of Dynasty XVII, several kings engaged the Hyksos in battle. Under Dynasty XVII's last king, Kamose, and Ahmose, the first king of the New Kingdom (ca. 1539–1070 B.C.), the Egyptians successfully pressured the last Hyksos king, Apepy, to leave his capital, Avaris, and eventually Egypt. Egyptian armies also retook Lower Nubia, setting the stage for ancient Egypt's imperial period.

Middle Kingdom and Second Intermediate Period

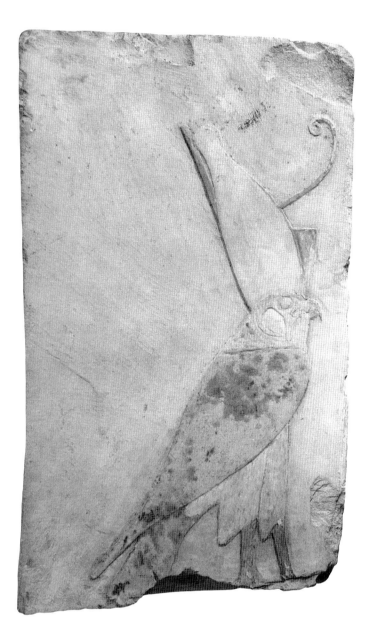

12.

Horus on a Temple Relief Fragment

(limestone, paint)

Dynasty XI, reign of Mentuhotep II (ca. 2025–1998 B.C.)
Deir el-Bahri
Length 48 cm; width 29 cm; thickness 16.4 cm
ACC. 3079-2

In the late nineteenth century, Edouard Naville's work at Deir el-Bahri focused not only on the great mortuary temple of Hatshepsut, but on a smaller, earlier temple belonging to Nebhotepre Mentuhotep (II). Mentuhotep II was responsible for the reunification of Egypt, the event that ended the First Intermediate Period (ca. 2025 B.C.) and led to the subsequent rehabilitation of the country. The traditional royal art centers that had ceased to exist during the First Intermediate Period were among the institutions Mentuhotep II resurrected. This fragment is a fine example of Dynasty XI craftsmanship from the royal workshop at Thebes.

This relief fragment, recovered from Mentuhotep II's mortuary temple, was probably part of a monumental scene representing the pharaoh.[1] A falcon wearing the Double Crown is delicately outlined in raised relief and represents Horus, ruler of Egypt, in his animal form. Horus was closely linked with the pharaoh during the king's earthly tenure as Egypt's ruler.

1. Personal communication with Brigitte Jaroš-Deckert, Vienna, Austria.

13.

Relief Fragment from Mentuhotep II's Temple

(limestone, paint)

Dynasty XI, reign of Mentuhotep II (ca. 2025–1998 B.C.)
Deir el-Bahri
Length 51 cm; width 25 cm; thickness 14 cm
ACC. 3079-1

During Dynasty IV (ca. 2675–2565 B.C.) of the Old Kingdom, pharaohs began to decorate the causeways and temple courtyards of their pyramid complexes. These early royal decorations featured both offering scenes and scenes of everyday life including agricultural activities, fishing and fowling, crafts, and leisure pastimes. These two basic forms of royal tomb decoration continued throughout the Old Kingdom, disappeared amid the turmoil of the

First Intermediate Period (ca. 2250–2025 B.C.), but emerged again during the reign of Mentuhotep II (ca. 2025–1998 B.C.), founder of the Middle Kingdom.

This relief segment, depicting most of the heads and upper torsos of four men, was recovered in excavations at Mentuhotep II's mortuary complex (see entry 12). The excavator's records indicate reliefs containing similar scenes were recovered from the building's southern side where the remains of its upper platform lay. The position of the men's arms and their closeness to one another suggest that they are involved in pulling closed a clapnet that would have been filled with ducks and geese.[1] This type of daily activity is a well-known decorative scheme in private chapels from the Old Kingdom through the Late Period. Traces of red paint survive on some of the bodies, and black paint can still be seen on the wigs. The feet in the upper right-hand corner belong to individuals once part of an upper register.

---

1. Personal communication with Brigitte Jaroš-Deckert, Vienna, Austria.

14.

Stela of Nakhty

(limestone, paint)

Dynasty XI (ca. 2025–1979 B.C.)
Provenience unknown
Height 95.3 cm; width 52.2 cm; thickness 20 cm
ACC. Z9-497

The ancient Egyptians frequently placed inscribed stone slabs called stelae in tomb chapels. The inscriptions on these funerary stelae generally identified the tomb owner's name and titles and often contained prayers for the granting of eternal gifts of food and drink. Stelae were usually located in the chapel built above the burial chamber so that the deceased's *ka* (spirit), housed in the mummy, had easy access to both the offerings mentioned in the inscription and gifts of food left by priests or members of the family.

The upper half of this stela records an inscription dedicated to the gods Osiris, Khentiamentiu, and Anubis. The inscription lists the categories of offerings that Nakhty (*nḥty*), this stela's owner, requested for his afterlife. Unlike most offering formulae, this one is very specific, identifying, for example, not just bread and beer but several types of bread and the variety of ale desired. Nakhty's titles are repeated several times so that we know he worked as an "Overseer of Cattle" (*imy-r k3w*) and a "Prophet" (*ḥm-nṯr*), that is, a priest of an unnamed temple.

In the first register, Nakhty faces right; he wears a kilt and a broad collar and holds a *sekhem* scepter of authority. Facing him from left to right are a full-sized man and three women. The man is dressed like Nakhty but sports a curled wig, while the women wear long sheath dresses and broad collars. The inscription identifies them as Nakhty's beloved son, Idiker (*id-iḵr*), and much-loved daughters, Punet (*pwn.t*), Senet-sobek (*sn.t-sbk*), and Punet (*pwn.t*) respectively. To the left of Idiker appears another man represented in a smaller scale because he is a servant. Called the "Herdsman" (*mniw*) Abkau (*ᶜb-k3w*), he

carries a jar and leads a gazelle. To the left on the second register, Nakhty and his wife share a seat, while inhaling sweet fragrances; Nakhty smells an ointment jar and his spouse sniffs a lotus. His wife's figure is badly damaged; her face is missing and her name largely destroyed with only the first two hieroglyphs (*ḥp*) remaining. Another ointment jar, a mirror in its case, a feather fan?, and a small chest rest beneath Nakhty's wife, all representing things she wanted in the next life. In front of the couple, a large offering table is ladened with desired food and drink. Large loaves of bread are capped by a haunch, head, and ribs of beef. Several other types of bread, lettuce, onions, a duck or goose, and a lotus are in the pile. Under the table are two jars of wine, while two others, with pointed seals, probably contained beer. To the right of the table, two more figures, servants, bear food offerings. The man is called the "Herdsman of Cattle" (*mniw iḥw*) Idu (*idw*) and the woman "Female Servant" (*ᶜky.t*)[1] Hetepu (*ḥtp.w*).

The offering formula, the style of carving, and the shape of many of the hieroglyphs date this stela to Dynasty XI. After it was carved, the stela was damaged, resulting in the loss of large chips of stone on the left side of lines 6, 7, 8, and 9 in the inscription and Nakhty's left arm in the first register. A second artisan reworked these damaged areas, although this second carving is similar to the original work. The different paint color on Nakhty's arm assists in indicating the existence of a second hand. Perhaps the stela was marred en route to the chapel or suffered damage shortly after being installed. The similarities in the styles between the repairs and the original work suggest a restoration during the time the stela was in use.

---

1. I have chosen to translate *ᶜky.t* as "servant." The term appears to designate someone who has entry to a normally inaccessible place such as a temple.

15.
Royal Funerary Boat
(cedar, paint)

Dynasty XII, reign of Senwosret III (ca. 1878–1859 B.C.)
Dashur
Length 9.2 m; width 2.3 m; depth 0.9 m
ACC. 1842-1

During his 1894–95 field season, Jacques de Morgan, a well-known French archaeologist, conducted excavations at Dashur, a site located about thirty-three kilometers south of Cairo. His work focused upon a pyramid complex containing the remains of a mud-brick pyramid that was once encased in stone, a mortuary temple, subsidiary burials, and enclosure walls. During these excavations, he recovered inscriptions identifying the pyramid as the burial place of Senwosret III, a powerful Dynasty XII pharaoh.

Following his exploration of the interior of the complex, de Morgan moved his work crews outside the southern wall. There he uncovered six(?)[1] wooden boat burials and a wooden sledge used in dragging the boats from the water across the sand to the pyramid complex. The boats' association with Senwosret III's pyramid complex suggest they belonged to him, but the lack of inscriptions prevents unquestionable identification of ownership.

The records concerning the Carnegie boat's provenience are sketchy. Its decided structural similarity to a boat in Chicago's Field Museum of Natural History and two boats in the Cairo Museum, all known to be from Dashur, indicates that the Carnegie boat was one of the six(?) discovered by de Morgan. Other factors also support a Dashur provenience.

The Dashur boats were part of a long tradition of boat use in ancient Egypt as well as a continuing association of boats (full-size vessels, models, and illustrations) with tombs. These boats' size, location, and number argue strongly against their identification as solar barques (boats buried for the king's use after his assimilation in the afterlife with the sun god, Re). Egyptologists do not even agree that boats or pits representing solar barques were ever part of royal burials. An alternative suggestion is that the Carnegie boat and its mates were buried in order to make riverine transport available to the king in his afterlife. If the boats were intended as royal traveling vessels, however, they should be more elaborate in style and construction and would most likely have been buried with greater formality adjacent to the pyramid, like Khufu's boats at Giza.

Based on analysis of the Carnegie boat's structure, the most likely explanation is that the Dashur boats were involved in some unknown manner in the burial ritual. The lack of mortises and tenons between plank ends within a strake (a single line of planking stretching the length of a boat) would have severely limited the Carnegie boat's ability to float. For a short time during a ritual, however, this boat *may* have been capable of floating. Most likely, then, these boats were towed across the Nile while carrying some of the burial equipment or cortege. As ritual equipment, the boats could not have been easily discarded, and their reuse in another ceremony would have been unlikely because of their weak structure. Therefore, the burials

alongside the pyramid complex's enclosure wall would correctly dispose of them as ritual equipment and, at the same time, make them available to the king, if needed, in the afterlife.

While the Carnegie boat was disassembled, several specialists studied its construction.[2] The boat was made from cedar cut into planks. Analysis located marks indicating that five different-sized adzes and a fine-toothed saw were used in shaping the boat's planks, which were assembled into strakes that were fastened to one another by mortises and tenons, and dovetails. Remnants of the paint used to mark the location of the mortises before carving have survived. Although this construction technique was a viable method for building riverine craft, the builders of the Dashur boats did not add enough mortises and tenons connecting the timbers to keep the boats together in the water for any extended period of time.

Steering oars are known from several of the Dashur boats, including the Carnegie example, but the boats did not have paddling oars or masts for sails. The ends of the boats turned up into papyriform finials that decayed while buried in the sand, and the end of the steering supports probably featured falcon heads. Research on all the boats indicates that blue or black, red, and white paint once decorated the hulls.

1. The excavation report is inconsistent about the number of boats excavated. The text says six while the maps only show five burials.

2. Cheryl Haldane and Richard Steffy, of the Institute of Nautical Archaeology in Austin, Texas, who analyzed the Carnegie boat while disassembled, provided the information on the boat's construction.

Middle Kingdom and Second Intermediate Period

16.

Model Boat

(gessoed wood, paint)

Dynasty XII (ca. 1979–1801 B.C.)
Provenience unknown
Boat: length 84.5 cm; height 30 cm; width 20 cm
ACC. 18121-1a through j

An ancient Egyptian commissioned a local artisan to build this model boat so that the owner could include it among his tomb furnishings. Detailed wooden models depicting activities such as traveling by boat, butchering cattle, working in a granary, baking bread, and brewing beer were often included in the funerary equipment of noblemen during the First Intermediate Period and Middle Kingdom. Daily life scenes painted or carved on the tomb walls functioned in the same manner from the late Old Kingdom (ca. 2565–2250 B.C.) through the New Kingdom (ca. 1539–1070 B.C.). Both the scenes and the models were made to surround the deceased with a familiar environment in the afterlife as well as to ensure that such activities known during the owner's lifetime would exist in the hereafter.

This model boat probably represented a traveling vessel although many of its accoutrements, including mast, rigging, and most sailors, have been lost. In addition, it is unclear whether the rudder post, six sailors and possible owner (one standing figure has a strap for attaching a false beard), and steering oar belong with this boat or were added recently from another model. Certainly the rudder post is suspect, but the single rudder oar appears to match this boat. This model may have been included among the funerary equipment to ensure that the tomb's owner could travel to the sacred site of Abydos after his death.

17.
Offering Table of Horweser

(fine-grained sandstone)

Dynasty XII (ca. 1979–1801 B.C.)
Abydos, Osiris temenos
Length 31.2 cm; width 27 cm; thickness 5.5 cm
ACC. 2231-3

The "Overseer of Sealers" *(imy-r sḏзw.tyw),* Horweser *(ḥr-wsr),* dedicated this small offering table to Osiris, who is called "lord of Busiris and Abydos and foremost of the Westerners." Offering tables like this and the one in entry 20 were made to provide the deceased with offerings needed throughout eternity. The offering formula, written in hieroglyphs, like those on many stelae, requests that the gods give bread, beer, cloth, linen, incense, and oil to the owner. The artist has supplemented the text with depictions of several types of bread, a leg of beef, and two beer jars. The text also mentions Horweser's mother's name, Sithathor *(sз.t-ḥwtḥr),* thereby indicating his family lineage. The formula, the carving, and the names all are characteristic of a Dynasty XII date.

Although Horweser's name was damaged in both places, enough remains to identify him. The sign meaning "weser" *(wsr)* is not written in true hieroglyphic form; the shape is, instead, a hieratic character, suggesting the craftsman was copying from a text in that cursive script.

Middle Kingdom and Second Intermediate Period

18.

Stela Belonging to Kemtu and His Wife It

(limestone, paint)

Dynasty XII (ca. 1979–1801 B.C.)
Provenience unknown
Height 73 cm; width 42 cm; thickness 14 cm
ACC. 21538-38

This stela is carved in shallow sunk relief, with remains of blue pigment preserved in the inscription; the cornice top was once brightly painted in alternating blue and red stripes. Its large size, its type of dedication formula, and the individuals remembered on it all indicate that it probably once stood near the processional way at Abydos. Dedicated to Abydos's two most popular gods Osiris, lord of the underworld, and Wepwawet, protector of the cemetery, the stela probably commemorated a pilgrimage made to Abydos by its owner, "Overseer of a Storehouse" (*imy-r šnꜥ.w*) Kemtu (*kmt.w*). By erecting this stela, Kemtu and all mentioned in its inscription could partake eternally in the sacred rituals at Abydos; the two eyes near the stela's top allowed the owner to observe forever.

Stelae frequently provide Egyptologists with informative geneologies that provide insight into the structure of ancient Egyptian families, in this case a "middle"-class one. The central figures on this example are Kemtu, seated in the upper left, and his wife, "Lady of the House" (*nbt pr*) It (*it*), in the upper right. The inscription tells us that Kemtu was the son of a woman, Khenty-Khety (*hnty-hty*), who was the daughter of Key (*ky*). It's mother, Sepenmut (*sp-n-mwt*), is also mentioned. The other

figures depicted on the stela are Kemtu and It's relatives or servants. These individuals are represented on a smaller scale to indicate the respect that they owed Kemtu and It. The man between Kemtu and It is "Majordomo of the Palace"[1] (*hry-pr n pr-ꜥꜣ*) Hepu (*hp.w*). From his position on the stela, he may be Kemtu's son by a different wife, Menkhet (*mnh.t*).

The second register contains two and possibly three more family members whose relationship to Kemtu is unclear. The woman is "Lady of the House" Key, a daughter of Sitmedjha (*sꜣ.t-mdh?*). Since she is named Key like Kemtu's grandmother, it is likely that she is a close family member, because Egyptians frequently revived a family member's name in alternating generations. The seated man on the left is Renefankh (*rn.f-ꜥnh*), the son of Key, a woman who was deceased. The smaller figure to his right is entitled "Majordomo" (*hry-pr*) Kebes (*kbs*), the son of Senaaib (*snꜥꜥ-ib*). The man presenting offerings to Key is a servant, "Majordomo" Isu (*isw*).

The lowest register represents servants of Kemtu and It. From the left, there is "Female Butler" (*wbꜣy.t*) Itwadjet (*it-wꜣd.t*) and then "Majordomo" (*hry-pr*) Werrensobek (*wr-rn-sbk*); the last servant has been lost along with the stela's corner.

---

1. "Majordomo" is the conventional term used by Egyptologists for men who are domestic servants.

Middle Kingdom and Second Intermediate Period

19.

Statue of Tety and His Family

(gabbro)

Dynasty XII (ca. 1979–1801 B.C.)
Abydos, x57
Height 71 cm; width 19 cm; depth 37 cm
ACC. 4558-2

This statue represents a seated man wearing a long skirt tied just below his chest. His hands rest palm down on his knees. Although most of his head is missing, the remains show that he wore a smooth shoulder-length wig. The style of dress indicates that the statue depicts a Middle Kingdom official. The hieroglyphic inscription, starting on his lap and running down the skirt's front between the hands, confirms this attribution. The brief offering formula indicates that the statue belonged to the "Senior Keeper of Nekhen" *(s3b ỉry nḫn)* Tety *(tỉty)*. His title is generally given to middle-ranking local officials.

Two figures appear on either side of Tety's lower legs. To his left, a woman stands upright, arms at her sides. She wears a simple sheath dress and large curled wig, a typical costume of Middle Kingdom women. The other figure is attired in a *shendyt* kilt and has a clean-shaven head. Both figures have a short inscription at the base of their feet that identify them. The woman is Tety's wife, "Lady of the House" *(nbt pr)* Itankh *(ỉt-ꜥnḫ);* the man is Tety's son, "Chief Administrator of the City" *(wꜥr.tw ꜥ3 n nỉw.t)* Ifet *(ỉft).* Both Itankh and Ifet are depicted in a smaller scale to show their relative importance to the statue's subject, Tety.

Representations on tomb walls, artifacts found in towns and cemeteries such as this statue, and certain written records give Egyptologists insights into daily life in ancient Egypt. The nuclear family was the fundamental unit in society, although the respect that children owed their parents throughout their lives often resulted in the sharing of a home among three generations. Marriages were generally arranged, but there was no formal ceremony. A couple moved in together after negotiating a contract identifying the possessions brought to the union by both parties; this protected each individual in the event of divorce. Adultery, infertility, or simply antipathy were all valid reasons for divorce, but because of its expense, divorce was rare.

20

The husband was responsible for supporting the family while the wife was expected to manage the home. Within any class of ancient Egyptian society, women held rights similar to men. They could own and dispose of property independently and initiate or testify at law proceedings, including divorce. Literate women are known among the upper class and a few held titles in local temples or government.

Children were the chief reason for marriage. Egyptians appear to have had large families because many children did not survive to adulthood. Very young children spent their day in play, although almost all illustrations show children at work when they are not standing with their parents. If they were lucky, by the age of six or seven children started school; otherwise they learned responsibilities that would enable them to earn a living as adults.

Children, identified by a sidelock of hair, nudity, and a finger in the mouth, are occasionally depicted with their parents in statues or tomb illustrations. In this statue, Ifet has an administrative title and wears an adult piece of clothing, the *shendyt* kilt.

20.

Offering Table

(limestone)

Dynasty XII-XIII (ca. 1979–1627/1606 B.C.)
Abydos, North Cemetery?
Length 55.7 cm; width 51.5 cm; thickness 9.5 cm
ACC. 4558-1

The ancient Egyptians developed several ways to guarantee the perpetual availability of food and other offerings to the dead. They inscribed and illustrated tomb walls, stelae, coffins, and offering tables with formulae and pictures designed to solve this problem. Offering tables, whether a simple ceramic tray with modeled clay food or an enormous stone slab with elaborate hieroglyphs and skillfully carved representations, served as eternal remembrances of the needs of the deceased.

Middle Kingdom and Second Intermediate Period

21

To Egyptologists, however, inscribed offering tables, such as this one, are most interesting for the biographical and genealogical information they provide. This offering table belonged to Memy *(mmy)* and his wife, "Lady of the House" *(nbt pr)* Senebtisy *(snb-tsy),* and was probably commissioned by her son, Amenhotep *(imn-ḥtp).* The hieroglyphs that would have clarified this point were omitted, however, because of a lack of space.

Although this offering table was found at Abydos, its inscription makes no mention of Osiris, chief god of this site. Rather, it invokes Geb, Anubis, Tefnut, Re, and Hathor. In addition to Memy and Senebtisy, four other individuals are mentioned: "Controller of the Phyle"[1] *(mty n s3)* Wadjkare *(rꜥ-w3d-k3),* "Controller of the Phyle" Sionuris *(s3-in-ḥr.t),* "Wab Priest" *(w3b)* Sobekhotep *(sbk-ḥtp),* and "Overseer of the Canal" *(imy-r mr)* Mentuhotep *(mn.tw-ḥtp).* Although there are no clues to the genealogical relationships among these men, this table does identify the responsibilities of four minor government officials during the Middle Kingdom.

---

1. A phyle was a group of priests responsible for certain temple functions over the period of one month, a service it repeated three times a year. Thus a temple had four phyles, each of which carried out identical responsibilities. This rotation system allowed for part-time priests; during the remaining nine months these men had other employment.

21.
Head of an Unidentified Official

(diabase)

Late Dynasty XII or Dynasty XIII (ca. 1878–1627/1606 B.C.)
Provenience unknown
Height 14 cm; width 10.5 cm
ACC. 9007-22

This head and upper torso was once part of a small statue depicting a minor official who was probably shown seated on a low-backed chair. The statue's nose, mouth, and chin have been severely battered. If the statue was ever inscribed, the man's name and title were lost when the piece was damaged. This object could have functioned either as a *ka* (spirit) statue of the official left in his tomb or as a votive offering to a deity in its temple.

When a statue or relief lacks an inscription and a provenience, Egyptologists must exploit other information to assist in dating the artifact. Art historians have studied the changes in the way the ancient Egyptian artisans depicted features and clothing on statues. The results of such research indicate that the wig type, the heavily lidded eyes, and the harsh wide mouth of this statue date to late Dynasty XII or Dynasty XIII.

22.
Stela of Senebsewemi and Renpetyef

(limestone)

Dynasty XIII (ca. 1801–1627/1606 B.C.)
Probably Abydos, North Cemetery
Height 54 cm; width 36 cm; thickness 6 cm
ACC. 2983-6701

This stela, carved in shallow sunk relief with little modeling, was dedicated to the gods "Osiris, foremost of the Westerners [the dead]," and "Wepwawet, lord of the necropolis." The primary inscription[1] mentions two men: "Overseer of the Seal" *(imy-r ḥtm)* Senebsewemi *(snb-sw-mꜥ)* and "Overseer of the Storehouse" *(imy-r st)* and "Overseer of the Seal" *(imy-r ḥtm)* Renpetyef *(rnpty.f).* In the first register, Renpetyef, to the right of center, presents food offerings to a seated Senebsewemi on the left. Their respective positions suggest that Senebsewemi is a

senior relative of the Renpetyef, but the inscription does not clarify this point. The woman at the far right, named Ity *(ìtì)*, was probably married to one of the two men in that register. The two men located at the far right of registers 2 and 3 may be relatives as well. They are Werneb-tawy *(wr-nb-twy)* in register 2 and another Senebsewemi in register 3. The latter's lack of titles and any indication that he is deceased implies that he was quite young when the stela was commissioned.

The remaining individuals were servants, probably of the elder Senebsewemi and Renpetyef. Some possess minor titles, such as "Butler" *(wdpw* and *wb3)*, "Skipper" *(nfw)*, and "Follower" *(šms.w)*. Although several of their names, such as Ptahhotep *(ptḥ-ḥtp)* and Kemtu *(kmt.w)*, are clearly of Egyptian origin, others might be northwest Semitic or Egyptian with northwest Semitic influence. These include Ibi *(ᶜbᶜ)*, Iawemniwt *(ì3w-m-nìw.t)*, Iaemankh *(ì3-m-ᶜnḫ)*, and Iwireri *(ìw.ì-rrì)*. The presence of Asiatic

servants on this stela conforms with evidence from other sources indicating that Asiatic immigrants entered Egypt in growing numbers throughout the Middle Kingdom, often finding employment in Egyptian households as domestics.

The dedication of the stela to Osiris and Wepwawet suggests an original location of Abydos, a site sacred to these two deities during the late Middle Kingdom. A stela in the Cairo Museum (CCG 20718), identical in style, belongs to another Senebsewemi, perhaps a grandfather or grandson of this stela's owner. The fact that the provenience of the Cairo Museum stela is the North Cemetery at Abydos suggests that this stela of Senebsewemi and Renpetyef should probably be assigned to the same location.

---

1. I want to thank Paul O'Rourke, of The Brooklyn Museum, for his assistance and insight in the reading of the names inscribed on this stela.

Middle Kingdom and Second Intermediate Period

23.
Amuletic Seals and Scarabs

23 a-g: *Clockwise from left*

a. Design Amulet
(glazed steatite)
First Intermediate Period
   (ca. 2250–2025 B.C.)
Hu, W176
Length 2 cm; width 1.2 cm
ACC. 2231-33

b. Design Amulet with Human
   Head
(faience)
Second Intermediate Period
   (ca. 1648–1539 B.C.)
Hu, Y438
Length 2.4 cm; width 1.7 cm
ACC. 1234-8

c. Design Amulet Depicting a
   Winged Scarab
(glazed steatite)
Second Intermediate Period–
   early Dynasty XVIII (ca. 1648–
   1425 B.C.)
Abydos, D102
Length 1.5 cm; width 1.1 cm
ACC. 1917-188

d. Scarab
(faience)
Second Intermediate Period–
   early Dynasty XVIII (ca. 1648–
   1425 B.C.)

Abydos, D102
Length 1.7 cm; width 1 cm
ACC. 1917-181

e. Scarab with Jumbled
   Hieroglyphs
(faience)
Second Intermediate Period–
   early Dynasty XVIII (ca. 1648–
   1425 B.C.)
Abydos, D71
Length 1.6 cm; width 1.2 cm
ACC. 1917-268

f. Name? Scarab
(faience)
Second Intermediate Period
   (ca. 1648–1539 B.C.)
Provenience unknown
Length 2 cm; width 1.4 cm
ACC. 11983-16e

g. Scarab Depicting a Lion
(glazed steatite)
Second Intermediate Period
   (ca. 1648–1539 B.C.)
Abydos
Length 1.8 cm; width 1.3 cm
ACC. 2231-32

Among the many objects people identify as typically Egyptian, amuletic seals and scarabs bearing designs form one of the largest groups. Although most popular from the Middle Kingdom through Dynasty XXVI (from ca. 2025 to 525 B.C.), this object type is recovered from late Old Kingdom through Ptolemaic Period (from ca. 2565 to 30 B.C.) contexts. Versions from the First Intermediate Period (ca. 2250–2025 B.C.) often have a ridge, shank, hemicylinder, or animal back and a naturalistic or geometric design base. The design amulet bearing a geo-

metric motif and a longitudinally pierced hemicylindrical back (figure 23a) is an example of this initial type. The earliest examples were probably used as amulets rather than seals, since they are found almost exclusively in funeral jewelry of women and children and the designs are not incised deeply enough to leave an impression in mud or wax.

During the First Intermediate Period, a new motif, the scarab beetle, came into use as a back type for many amulets. Shortly thereafter, the scarab became the most common type of back for both amuletic and functional seals. The beetle's form was easily incorporated into the shapes already in use. Its widespread popularity, however, grew from the concepts symbolized by the scarab. In writing, the hieroglyph of a scarab beetle embodied the words "become" or "come into existence." This association developed because the ancient Egyptians watched the beetle's young appear, seemingly spontaneously, from the ground. They did not know, of course, that the adult scarab beetle had previously deposited eggs in a dung ball in its nest underground.

Additionally, the scarab was linked with Re, the sun god. In fact, the scarab beetle represented Khepri, Re's morning aspect. This connection developed because the living beetle, after selecting a piece of dung for food, packs the dung into a ball by pushing it back and forth across the ground before depositing it in its lair for future consumption. The ancient Egyptians identified the resulting sphere with the sun disk. Therefore, to them a giant scarab beetle guided the sun across the sky. With these powerful connections, it is not surprising that the scarab was an extremely popular amuletic symbol.

The remaining six amuletic seals and scarabs represent a range of Second Intermediate Period back types (figures 23b-d) and common base designs (figures 23e-g). Figure 23d illustrates a version of a scarab back representative of this period. The other two back types (figures 23b and c) are rarer. Second Intermediate Period base designs on scarabs and other amulets include hieroglyphs (figure 23e), proper names (figure 23f), and animals and humans (figure 23g).

Although figures 23c and d illustrate Second Intermediate Period designs, their provenience, a private tomb at Abydos, clearly supports an early Dynasty XVIII (ca. 1479–1425 B.C.) date during the reigns of Hatshepsut and Tuthmosis III. This inconsistency can be explained in two ways: either the designs on these amulets continued to be manufactured into the early New Kingdom or the objects were heirlooms kept by a family years after their original production.

24.

Objects of the Pan-grave Culture

Second Intermediate Period (ca. 1648–1539 B.C.)

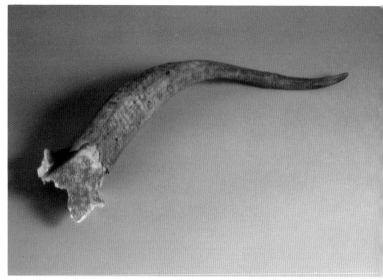

24a

24b

a. Decorated Horn	*b.* Pieces of a Bracelet
(sheep or goat horn and bone,	(shell)
paint)	Provenience unknown
Provenience unknown	Each rectangle: length approx.
Length 31.1 cm; width of horn	2.5 cm; width approx. 0.7 cm
4 cm	ACC. 9074-2337
ACC. 9074-2577	

At some point in Dynasty XIII (1801–1627/1606 B.C.), Egypt was subjected to an influx of foreigners for the first time in its history. In Lower Egypt, the Hyksos from Palestine infiltrated the Delta, eventually establishing a dynasty that lasted nearly a hundred years. In Upper Egypt, people, probably from the Eastern Desert in Nubia, immigrated into the Nile Valley in small groups. Early archaeologists called these desert people Pan-grave because their graves, when eroded, appeared as shallow pan-like depressions in the desert.

These graves contain an interesting mix of artifacts. Many objects, such as pottery and decorated horns from cattle, sheep, goat, and gazelle, have strong affinities with Nubian cultures of that general era. At the same time, many burials exhibit Egyptian weapons and occasionally gold jewelry. Given the mix of Nubian and Egyptian objects and the frequency of weaponry, Egyptologists have generally accepted that the Pan-grave people may have been the Medjay, mercenaries famed in ancient Egypt as police and soldiers.

The sheep or goat horn (figure 24a), decorated with spots of red ocher, is one of several types of animal horns often found in caches near Pan-grave burials. Although the exact use of these horns is unknown, their large numbers suggest that pastoralism and the hunting of desert game played important roles in the Pan-grave people's subsistence. Figure 24b depicts a rare example of Pan-grave jewelry; these mother-of-pearl rectangles would have been lashed together.

25 a-c: Left to right

25.

Female Figurines

a. (ceramic)
Second Intermediate Period
  (ca. 1648–1539 B.C.)
Abydos, D28a
Height 12.1 cm; width 4.8 cm
ACC. 1662-41

b. (mud)
Second Intermediate Period–
  early Dynasty XVIII (ca. 1648–
  1425 B.C.)
Abydos, D119

Height 6.6 cm; width 2.3 cm;
  thickness 1.5 cm
ACC. 1917-234

c. (limestone, paint)
Dynasty XIII–XVII (ca. 1801–
  1539 B.C.)
Abydos, D92
Height 9.8 cm; width 3.8 cm
ACC. 1917-107

The ancient Egyptians considered the transition from death to rebirth a treacherous journey. To aid the deceased, they included among the funerary equipment various magical objects such as these three female figurines. Each of these figures has abbreviated or schematically modeled limbs and two possess highly stylized heads. The head of figure 25c is missing, but probably would have been different from the others, since comparison with similar statues that are fully preserved shows that it would have had recognizable facial features. The lack of detail on the other two heads and on all of the limbs serves to emphasize the dominant feminine attributes of each figure. To the ancient Egyptians, a woman's breasts and genitalia were intimately tied with her fertility, and figures with accentuated sexual attributes evoked the concepts of fertility and birth. The presence of such potent feminine imagery would have assisted the deceased in his or her transition through spiritual and physical rebirth into the afterlife.

Figures 25a and c are well-known types. The latter is especially interesting because the black dots encircling the wrist and arm and running down the figurine's middle, along with the crosses around the abdomen, represent tatoos. The triangular patch of dots is a rendering of pubic hair. The markings on the arms probably depict bracelets, while the crosses may be a decorative girdle. Tatoos on figurines may be a way of emphasizing female sexuality. It is interesting to note that body decorations are never illustrated on women depicted in tomb or temple reliefs.

Figure 25b is more unusual. Parallels are known from other sites in Egypt,[1] and although this type of figurine is often dated to the Middle Kingdom, it is more likely that these figurines belong to the Second Intermediate Period. Note this figurine's rectangular shape, the flattened head decorated with a circle of incised dots (not visible), the small cone-like breasts, and the schematically rendered facial features and genitalia. These characteristics were common on Near Eastern and Aegean figurines, especially in Mycenaean Greece and Syro-Palestine, before they appeared on figurines in Egypt. As a result of increasing contact with Near Eastern cultures in the late Middle Kingdom and Second Intermediate Period, the Egyptians borrowed this type of figurine or applied their own stylistic features to well-known Near Eastern types. These characteristic features continued on, at least in Palestine,[2] after their popularity waned in Egypt.

This mud figurine also exhibits one very unusual feature.[3] Generally, the pubic area on these figures is outlined by a triangular patch of incised dots similar to the painted pubes on figure 25c. On this figurine, however, in addition to the dots there is a semicircle of applied clay representing the female genitalia. Within this semicircle, a small round circle of clay emerges. This appears to be a very rare representation of a woman giving birth, which is in keeping with the interpretation that this figure is a fertility or rebirth symbol.

1. B. Bruyère, *Rapport sur les fouilles de Deir el Medineh (1934–1935),* Fouilles de l'Institut Français d'Archéologie Orientale du Caire, 16 (1939): 143–44.

2. Refer to the Ashdod figurine of a Philistine goddess discussed in M. Dothan, *Ashdod II–III* (Jerusalem: The Department of Antiquities and Museums in the Ministry of Education and Culture, The Department of Archaeology, Hebrew University, and The Israel Exploration Society, 1971), pp. 129–30.

3. I want to thank Richard Fazzini, The Brooklyn Museum, for suggesting this possibility.

Middle Kingdom and Second Intermediate Period

26.

Relief Fragment Inscribed
with a Cartouche of Queen Neferyt

(indurated limestone)

Probably Dynasty XVII (ca. 1627/1606–1539 B.C.)
Provenience unknown
Length 18 cm; width 16.3 cm
ACC. 29691-216

This fragment probably was once part of a temple relief. Although the inscription is short, it is interesting because the royal name inside the oval (known as a cartouche) belongs to a previously unknown queen. Her name can be translated as "Neferyt" *(nfryt)* or "Neferyti" *(nfryti)* since the *ti* may have been used as an alternative writing of the feminine *t*. "Neferyti" has no known parallels, but "Neferyt" is a Middle Kingdom name. "Neferet" and its variants are common female names found in Old Kingdom through New Kingdom sources. By Dynasty XIII (ca. 1801 B.C.), certain royal women had acquired the privilege of placing their names inside cartouches.

The queen's title (located to the left of the cartouche) reads "One Who Is United with the Beautiful White Crown" *(ḫnm.t nfr ḥḏ.t)*. This phrase associates the queen with Nekhbet, the vulture goddess. Nekhbet symbolized Upper Egypt and, therefore, was identified with the White Crown, another symbol of the region. Since queens often wore a vulture-shaped crown, this title represented an-

other way of joining the queen to the goddess. Titles belonging to queens allow Egyptologists to study the patterns of Egyptian queenship. A queen was necessary to the king, not only as mother of future heirs to the throne, but as an integral part of the symbolic nature of ancient Egypt kingship.

This particular title is associated only with queens living between early Dynasty XII and early Dynasty XVIII (between ca. 1979 and 1457 B.C.). This piece's relief style, shallow carving, and lack of detail, however, support a narrower date of Dynasty XVII (ca. 1627/1606–1539 B.C.). Therefore, a synthesis of all the chronological information available from the fragment suggests a Dynasty XVII date for this queen's reign.

There are two queens from Dynasty XVII whose titles have been recovered but whose names are missing. One of these women, Intef the Elder's mother, bore the same title as this queen. A possibility exists that the fragment records the identity of this previously unnamed queen, the mother of Intef, although confirmation must wait upon additional archaeological or textual finds.[1]

---

1. I want to thank Dr. Lana Troy, Research Assistant, Institute of Egyptology, Uppsala University, Sweden, for suggesting this possibility.

New Kingdom, CIRCA 1539–1070 B.C.

INTRODUCTION

After he secured Egypt's borders by expelling the Hyksos and Kushites, Ahmose, the first king of the New Kingdom (Dynasty XVIII–XX, ca. 1539–1070 B.C.), reorganized the administration, placing loyal followers in the provincial offices once again under Egyptian control. The reforms he instituted in the administration and his revival of the economy, assisted by ambitious building programs, were to last for five hundred years. Ahmose's successors, such as Tuthmosis I and Tuthmosis III, were strong military leaders who spent their reigns extending the Egyptian empire by acquiring foreign territory. By about 1450 B.C., Egypt successfully claimed an empire extending from southern Syria, including most of Syro-Palestine, to the Nile's fourth cataract in Nubia. While a co-regent with Tuthmosis III, Hatshepsut, Egypt's highly successful female king, rebuilt many of the temples destroyed during the Second Intermediate Period (ca. 1648–1539 B.C.). During their reign, income from foreign gifts, tribute, and trade poured into the royal coffers, providing luxury for many people. Simultaneously, temples acquired extreme wealth from payments extracted by the Egyptian government from its foreign territories. This affluence gave the High Priest of Amun-Re increasing power that would eventually encourage competition against the king.

By the middle of Dynasty XVIII under Amenhotep III, Egypt was the wealthiest country in the ancient world. For unknown reasons, his successor, Amenhotep IV (Akhenaten), chose to break with the religious tradition that, according to official teaching, was responsible for Egypt's achievements. His new religion emphasized the Aten disk, an obscure manifestation of the sun god, and he elevated Aten's worship to an unprecedented level. Except for the glorification of Akhenaten and his wife, Nefertiti, who played an important part in the Aten cult, no other gods were recognized after his fifth regnal year and their temples were closed. Ensconced in a new capital, Akhetaten, now called el-Amarna, in Middle Egypt, Akhenaten focused on his religion and family, while ignoring most of the country's problems, including those within the foreign territories. Although indifferent to Egypt and its empire, Akhenaten controlled the country for seventeen years through the force of his personality. Following his death, first young Tutankhamen and, later, Horemheb returned Egypt to its cultural traditions.

With the death of Horemheb (ca. 1295 B.C.), a new family gained control. The succeeding era is known as the Ramesside Period (Dynasty XIX–XX, ca. 1295–1070 B.C.), so named because most of its kings were called Ramesses. The most successful rulers were Sety I and his son, Ramesses II (Dynasty XIX). Strong military leaders, they regained some foreign territory lost under Akhenaten while restrengthening the economy. Their building programs were ambitious: Abu Simbel, the Ramesseum, the hypostyle hall of the temple at Karnak, and several temples at Abydos are just a few achievements of their reigns. Ramesses II was succeeded by weak rulers, and in Dynasty XX, Egypt's last effective military leader, Ramesses III, was crowned. Imitating his famous namesake Ramesses II, he tried to hold onto Egypt's foreign territories while managing domestic problems. He was not wholly successful, however. The ancient records show the economy was in a serious decline, and his reign may have ended abruptly with his assassination. The dynasty's final rulers were ineffective kings barely able to protect Egypt's borders.

27a-f: Left to right

27.

Set of Dishes

(ceramic, paint)
Early Dynasty XVIII, reign of Tuthmosis III (ca. 1479–
   1425 B.C.)

a. Jug with a Handle
Abydos, D102
Height 14.8 cm; diameter 8.3 cm
ACC. 1917-500

b. Mug
Abydos, D102
Height 14.3 cm; diameter 4.6 cm
ACC. 1917-383

c. Large Jar
Abydos, D116
Height 28.5 cm; diameter 9.5 cm
ACC. 1917-413

d. Small Jar
Abydos, D102
Height 7.8 cm; diameter 5.5 cm
ACC. 1917-510

e. Large Bowl
Abydos, D102
Height 9.2 cm; diameter 29.8 cm
ACC. 1917-496

f. Shallow Ring-Base Bowl
Abydos, D119
Height 4.2 cm; diameter 12 cm
ACC. 1917-417

The ancient Egyptians used clay to form many items, but none were more common or necessary than the vessels for storing or serving food. Beginning in the early Predynastic Period (ca. 4500 B.C.) and continuing throughout Egyptian history, ceramic jars, often filled with food

offerings, were regularly left in tombs. In addition, thousands of sherds, the remains of everyday vessels, have been recovered from settlement sites such as el-Amarna, Kahun, and Deir el-Medina. Illustrations from tomb and temple walls also supply information on the variety and quantity of pottery containers used by the Egyptians.

In the New Kingdom, typical food containers included large vessels, small jars, wide shallow bowls, small bowls, jugs, and cylindrical mugs; the shapes of each were somewhat variable. Large jars such as figure 27c held grain, oil, beer, or perhaps wine, and immense storage jars and amphorae have been found as well. Most of the large jars had pointed bases so that they could not stand on their own. Therefore, these vessels were placed either in holes in the mud floor of a house or in pot stands of clay or wood. Occasionally representations of these vessels show them simply leaning against a convenient wall. Wide shallow bowls, for example, figure 27e, bore food either in the kitchen or on a banquet table. Eggs, bread, fruits (including grapes, pomegranates, dates, and figs), vegetables (such as lettuce, onions, garlic, turnips, and beans), or butchered beef, fish, or fowl were often placed in these large bowls. Small jugs like figure 27a probably held beer, wine, or water at a table, whereas figure 27b, a mug, and figure 27f, a small bowl, were employed as drinking glasses. Small jars such as figure 27d are very common although what they contained is uncertain; but most likely they functioned as a jug without a handle.

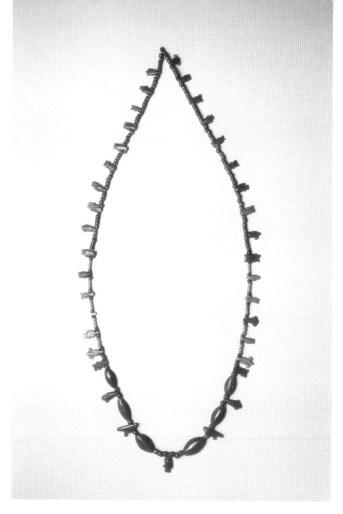

28. Detail

28.

Necklace with Amulets

(jasper, turquoise, faience)

Early Dynasty XVIII, reign of Tuthmosis III (ca. 1479–1425 B.C.)
Abydos, D102
Length 29 cm; most amulets: length 1 cm; width 0.5 cm
ACC. 1917-144

The Egyptian craftsman who fashioned this striking neck-lace mastered the techniques of working in hard stone. Simple ball beads, along with six cowrie-shaped ones, compose most of the necklace. Spaced among the beads are amulets representing the Bes-image, Taweret, and Horus (all deities popular with many Egyptians) and fish. The most common amulets, however, are lotus flowers, symbols of rebirth. Single-strand necklaces were always popular in ancient Egypt and are often recovered among grave goods. The quality of this piece, its excellent condi-tion, and the numerous amulets suggest that it was made specifically to protect its owner in the hereafter.

New Kingdom

43

29.

Kohl Tube in the Shape of a Monkey

(fine-grained limestone, paint)

Early Dynasty XVIII, reigns of Hatshepsut and Tuthmosis III
 (ca. 1479–1425 B.C.)
Abydos, D116
Height 9.3 cm; width 3 cm; depth 6 cm
ACC. 1917-2

In ancient Egypt, the widespread use of kohl or eye makeup was reflected in the production of great numbers of small kohl pots. These jars had a multitude of shapes. Cosmetic containers, either modeled in the form of monkeys or using monkeys as decorative elements, were present among funerary equipment from the late Old Kingdom through the end of the New Kingdom (from ca. 2345 to 1070 B.C.). Since monkeys, probably guenons imported from central Africa, were common pets, their frequent appearance on objects used in daily life is hardly surprising. Tomb paintings show pet monkeys entertaining their owners with their antics and occasionally harvesting ripe fruit for their masters.

This kohl jar is in the form of a pet monkey standing on its hind legs holding a small cylinder between its hands. The status of pet is easily indicated by the decorated collars encircling the animal's neck and lower body. Small marks filled with paint on its chest and back indicate areas of thicker fur. On the cylinder's front, Taweret, a well-known goddess, is schematically rendered. She is a deity depicting a pregnant hippopotamus with additional body parts from a woman, a lion, and a crocodile. Taweret's presence on this kohl jar follows her role as a popular household deity whose powers included guarding family members, particularly pregnant women or women undergoing childbirth.

30a-e: Left to right

30.

Group of Unusual Vessels

(ceramic, paint)
Early Dynasty XVIII, reigns of Hatshepsut and Tuthmosis III (ca. 1479–1425 B.C.)
Abydos, D116

---

a. Small Shouldered Jar
Height 7.6 cm; diameter 2.4 cm
ACC. 1917-401

b. Drinking Bowl?
Height 7.5 cm; diameter 6.8 cm
ACC. 1917-474

c. Amphora Jar
Height 12.2 cm; diameter 4.5 cm
ACC. 1917-404

d. Small Shouldered Jar
Height 7.5 cm; diameter 2.5 cm
ACC. 1917-410

e. Jug with Hieroglyphs
Height 9.8 cm; diameter 2.2 cm
ACC. 1917-403

During 1901, A.C. Mace excavated an early Dynasty XVIII necropolis in the northern cemetery zone at Abydos. Analysis of the tombs' contents indicates that the owners were comfortably circumstanced members of the "middle" class. Found in one tomb, these five vessels represent an unusual group of ceramics. Their small size and thorough surface polish suggest that all of these pieces were designed to contain liquids, probably precious oils or ointments. The clay indicates that they were made in Egypt, but their shapes and decorative elements are clearly non-Egyptian. The forms and ornamentation have elements similar to Syro-Palestinian, Cypriot, and Aegean vessels, but none is a true copy of a foreign ware.

In the New Kingdom, Egyptians increased contact with cultures outside of the Nile Valley. Their interest in the material culture of these foreigners is clearly observable in the objects from royal and noble tombs as well as those of the "middle" class. Perhaps these vessels are the result of a craftsman imitating shapes and styles seen briefly while in Syro-Palestine or observed on jars filled with imported substances traded into Egypt from that area. Other objects in this tomb show strong ties to the Levant.

Figure 30e is particularly interesting. Like the others, its ware is Egyptian, but its shape and the decorative elements of stripes and concentric circles imitate Cypriot designs. Egyptian hieroglyphs appear in red paint on opposite sides of the neck: *kꜣ* (𓂓) on one side and *ms* (𓄟) on the other, below the handle. Combined these glyphs do not translate into any recognizable version of a personal name or a meaningful word. The alternative is to suggest a translation of these words as a sentence, "May the *ka* [spirit] be born." This would connect the jar's contents with childbirth. Jars containing oils used during the birthing process are known from other contexts.

31a-c

31d

31.
Earrings

a. Leech-type Earrings
(gold, paste)
Early Dynasty XVIII, reigns of
  Hatshepsut and Tuthmosis III
  (ca. 1479–1425 B.C.)
Abydos, D116
Height 1.5 cm; width 1.4 cm
ACC. 1917-49
Height 1.6 cm; width 1.4 cm
ACC. 1917-50

b. Ribbed Penannular Earrings
(gold)
Early Dynasty XVIII, reign of
  Tuthmosis III (ca. 1479–
  1425 B.C.)
Abydos, D102
Diameter approx. 2 cm;
  thickness 0.8 cm
ACC. 1917-152
Diameter approx. 2 cm;
  thickness 0.9 cm
ACC. 1917-154

c. Penannular Earrings
(silver or electrum, paste)
Early Dynasty XVIII, reign of
  Tuthmosis III (ca. 1479–
  1425 B.C.)
Abydos, D102
Each: diameter 2 cm; thickness
  0.7 cm
ACC. 1917-155
ACC. 1917-156

d. Ear Studs
(glass)
Dynasty XVIII (ca. 1539–
  1295 B.C.)
Provenience unknown
Diameter 1.8 cm; length 3.1 cm
ACC. Z9-498a
Diameter 1.6 cm; length 3 cm
ACC. Z9-498b

Personal ornamentation was always popular among the ancient Egyptians. Sculptures and wall decorations often illustrate people wearing necklaces, bracelets, pectorals, and diadems. Earrings, however, were not common until after the Second Intermediate Period (ca. 1648–1539 B.C.). During this period and into the beginning of Dynasty XVIII (ca. 1539–1425 B.C.), the Egyptians' contacts with foreigners who wore this style of jewelry multiplied dramatically, probably accounting for its increased frequency in Egypt.

Hoops, studs, and plugs were the most common earring styles. Figure 31b displays hoops made from four triangular tubes, decoratively etched with lines. The four tubes were soldered together and bent into the hoop shape, giving the appearance of the inner section of an accordion. The two middle tubes are slightly longer and went through holes in the ears. Figure 31c represents a simpler hoop style that slid onto the earlobe. On this pair, the slit appears too small for regular use so perhaps these were made only as funerary accoutrements. Leech-type hoops (figure 31a) were a very common style and this pair is the earliest currently known. They were crafted by laying metal foil, here a reddish gold, over a paste core. The thin gold wires allowed the earrings to hang properly. To wear the colorful glass studs (figure 31d), another well-known type, the shaft was simply pushed through a hole in the earlobe to display the flattened circular head. Threads of white and dark blue glass decorate the shaft while turquoise-colored glass outlines the dark blue center of the head.

32.

Jug with a Lotus-Pattern Handle

(bronze)

Early Dynasty XVIII, reigns of Hatshepsut and Tuthmosis III
 (ca. 1479–1425 B.C.)
Abydos, D116
Height 8.8 cm; diameter 6 cm
ACC. 1917-54

Until the Middle Kingdom (ca. 2025 B.C.), copper was the strongest metal available to the ancient Egyptians. Smelted copper was most often melted in crucibles over open fires and the molten metal poured into stone or clay molds to make objects. Eventually craftsmen acquired from western Asia the technology and a raw material (tin) necessary for making bronze. Subsequently, bronze became the most common material for weapons and tools, and was also used for doors, vessels, statuettes, and personal ornaments. Workers could hammer bronze into sheets or cast it like copper in stone or clay molds. Small objects were also cast using the lost-wax process, but large objects were often cast around a core of sand and organic material.

An ancient Egyptian artisan shaped this jug by cold-hammering a bronze sheet over a form which could have been of wood, pottery, or stone. He finished its rim by folding the jug's edge over a length of wire. The handle, incised with a lotus flower design, was riveted to the body in three places near the rim and once on the shoulder. Originally, this jug probably featured a high polish achieved by burnishing the surface with a smooth stone.

32

32. Detail of handle

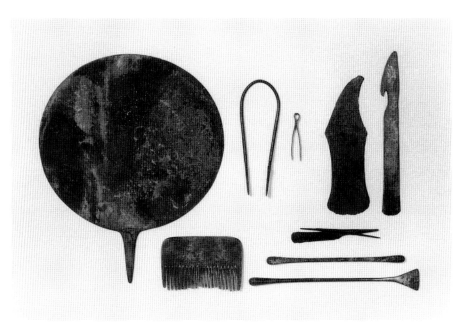

33.
Toilette Equipment

33a-i: Clockwise from left

a. Mirror with Its Handle
  Missing
(bronze)
Early Dynasty XVIII, reigns of
  Hatshepsut and Tuthmosis III
  (ca. 1479–1425 B.C.)
Abydos, D116
Length 20.2 cm; width 16.8 cm
ACC. 1917-14

b and c. Tweezers
(bronze)
Early Dynasty XVIII, reign of
  Tuthmosis II (ca. 1479–
  1425 B.C.)
Abydos, D119

Length 10.5 cm; width 3.8 cm
ACC. 1917-231 (large)
Length 4.4 cm; width 1 cm
ACC. 1917-231a (small)

d and e. Razors
(bronze)
Early Dynasty XVIII, reign of
  Tuthmosis III (ca. 1479–
  1425 B.C.)
Abydos, D116
Length 12.5 cm; width 4 cm
ACC. 1917-17
Abydos, D102
Length 14.6 cm; width 1.7 cm
ACC. 1917-17a

f. Hair Implement
(bronze)
Dynasty XVIII (ca. 1539–
  1295 B.C.)
Hu, Y53
Length 8.2.cm; width 1.5 cm
ACC. 1234-16

g and h. Kohl Sticks
(bronze)
Early Dynasty XVIII, reigns of
  Hatshepsut and Tuthmosis III
  (ca. 1479–1425 B.C.)
Abydos, D116
Length 12.5 cm; diameter
  0.8 cm

ACC. 1917-6
Length 15.5 cm; width 2 cm
ACC. 1917-21

i. Comb
(horn)
Early Dynasty XVIII, reigns of
  Hatshepsut and Tuthmosis III
  (ca. 1479–1425 B.C.)
Abydos, D116
Length 7.5 cm; width 5 cm
ACC. 1917-24

Cleanliness was very important to the ancient Egyptians, who practiced a daily toilette including frequent bathing. Since hairiness was considered slovenly, facial and most body hair was shaved regularly. The only exceptions were the small mustaches or short beards sported by noblemen and the stubble found on the faces of men during mourning. Men and women regularly cut their hair, styled their wigs if they wore them, and applied makeup, most commonly eye paint. Tomb scenes depict individuals as well as professional barbers and hairdressers using toilette implements easily recognizable today.

Mirrors (figure 33a) were common. When excavated, this mirror's handle was not found, suggesting it was made of wood and had decayed. The shape of ancient Egyptian mirrors imitated the sun, thus giving them a sym-bolic as well as functional importance. Razors, in several shapes (e.g., figures 33d and e), were employed to remove unwanted facial hair and to shave the head. Some razors similar to figure 33d had bronze or wood handles riveted to the blade's midsection so that the blade could be manipulated more easily. Everybody wore eye paint, today called kohl, for cosmetic, medicinal, and practical reasons. The variability in size and design of kohl containers caused kohl sticks (figures 33g and h) to be fashioned in several styles and dimensions. Figure 33f is called a hair implement because we are unsure of the object's true function. Often found accompanying other pieces of toilette equipment, such objects have been called razors and wig curlers, although neither function fits this implement. In all likelihood, they served several purposes.

34.

Foreign Vessels

a. "Pilgrim Flask"
(ceramic, paint)
Early Dynasty XVIII, reigns of
 Hatshepsut and Tuthmosis III
 (ca. 1479–1425 B.C.)
Abydos, D116
Height 11.3 cm; diameter 5 cm
ACC. 1917-407

b. Juglet
(ceramic)
Early Dynasty XVIII, reign of
 Tuthmosis III (ca. 1479–
 1425 B.C.)
Abydos, D102
Height 15 cm; diameter 4.7 cm
ACC. 1917-512

c. Spindle Bottle
(ceramic)
Early Dynasty XVIII, reign of
 Tuthmosis III (ca. 1479–
 1425 B.C.)
Abydos, D102
Height 31 cm; diameter 2 cm
ACC. 1917-525

d. Bilbil (Base-ring Ware Juglet)
(ceramic)
Dynasty XVIII (ca. 1539–
 1295 B.C.)
Abydos?, D111
Height 15 cm; diameter 3 cm
ACC. 21537-49

34 a-d: Left to right

The deserts flanking the Nile Valley provided a natural barrier that isolated the ancient Egyptians from other cultures. Nevertheless, the Egyptians always maintained contact with other populations, including those from Mesopotamia, Palestine, the Aegean Islands, Libya, and Nubia. They traditionally considered all people not living in the Nile Valley, speaking Egyptian, and practicing Egyptian culture to be foreigners; even the nomads from the adjacent deserts were outsiders. The ancient Egyptians generally discouraged foreigners from entering Egypt except as war captives, although after about 1550 B.C. this attitude shifted and increasing numbers of immigrants settled in Egypt and became acculturated. Foreigners could become "Egyptian" if they adopted the characteristics the ancient Egyptians used to identify themselves.

Prior to the Middle Kingdom (ca. 2025 B.C.), interaction between Egypt and the rest of the ancient world was largely the result of erratically conducted trade. During the Middle Kingdom, foreign contacts increased steadily; the Egyptians expanded trade with the Aegean peoples and the Puntites, while deploying a more organized army to exact tribute in finished and raw materials from Syro-Palestine and Nubia. The military ambitions and achievements of the early kings of Dynasty XVIII (ca. 1539–1425 B.C.) led to the acquisition of an empire extending from southern Anatolia to the fourth cataract in Nubia. This expansion continued to intensify Egyptian contact with foreign cultures, bringing new technol-

ogy, goods, and people into a civilization that had previously been largely isolated. This trend continued throughout Dynasty XVIII (ca. 1539–1295 B.C.), flourishing under Pharaoh Amenhotep III, when Egypt was the wealthiest country in the ancient world. After the isolation ceased, foreign cultures played an increasingly prominent role in Egyptian history. Eventually the country fell to a succession of foreigners, including the Kushites, Assyrians, Persians, and Greeks.

These four vessels are typical examples of foreign vessels used as containers for imported goods during early Dynasty XVIII (ca. 1539–1425 B.C.), when Egypt was aggressively expanding in the Near East. The small size of the containers, their dense surface finish achieved by polishing, the narrow necks and mouths, and the handles suggest that all these vessels were intended to carry costly, volatile liquids. Figures 34b and c are typical examples of Syrian vessels probably used to export perfume and aromatic resins respectively. The *bilbil* (figure 34d), which comes from Cyprus, may have held a solution containing opium, although this identification remains unproven. Figure 34a is an Egyptian copy of a pottery shape whose original source was Syro-Palestine or Mycenae. The term "pilgrim flask" was originally given to vessels of a much later date, but is now used to describe all two-handled, lenticular flasks.

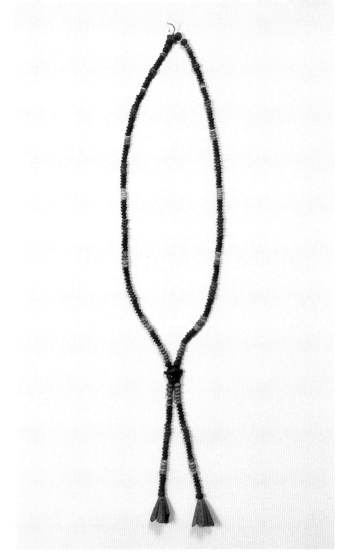

35.
Necklace with Tassels
(faience)

Early Dynasty XVIII, reigns of Hatshepsut and Tuthmosis III
  (ca. 1539–1425 B.C.)
Abydos, D116
Length 88 cm
ACC. 1917-30

This necklace is composed of faience, a man-made material that the Egyptians developed as early as 3000 B.C. Faience is made up of a ground quartz (sand) core that is bound together with a substance most likely to be natron (hydrated sodium carbonate) or salt and water; a finished piece of faience always has a glaze over its core. Although the Egyptians modeled faience and turned it like pottery, artisans most commonly formed it in molds because it is very malleable. Thus, faience was an ideal substance for the manufacture of beads, amulets, figurines, and small vessels.

After a faience piece had been molded and dried, it was glazed and then fired in simple kilns. The Egyptians developed three methods for glazing faience: efflorescence, where the glaze was incorporated into the matrix; slurry, a runny glaze that was painted on an object's surface; and occasionally cementation, where the object was buried in a powder which melted and glazed the piece during firing. Firing always brought out the glaze's color. A bright, blue-green was the most popular color and was often believed to have protective powers. It imitated turquoise, a stone precious to the Egyptians, but in short supply. Objects in dark red, dark blue, yellow, green, or white faience are also known.

Quartz was easily obtained from the sand of the low desert; natron came from several large deposits within Egypt, such as Wadi Natron, northwest of the Delta. The ease with which the components of faience were found kept this material affordable to even the poorest in Egyptian society. However, the wealthy often used it as well. Tutankhamen, a Dynasty XVIII pharaoh, possessed several faience necklaces imitating floral wreaths.

35. Detail

This necklace and another similar one (with steatite and gold as well as faience beads) in the Carnegie collection were recovered from a large tomb group at Abydos. The single-strand necklace of turquoise-blue, dark blue, dark red, and yellow beads is strung through a leopard-head bead spacer to form a loop that went around the wearer's neck. Each end of the necklace was finished in a tassel shaped like a jasmine blossom that hung free.

36.
Triple Kohl Tube

(wood, ivory?)

Early Dynasty XVIII, reigns of Hatshepsut and Tuthmosis III
 (ca. 1479–1425 B.C.)
Abydos, D116
Height 15.5 cm; width 7.5 cm
ACC. 1917-4

This multiple kohl tube, designed to hold three separate measures of eye paint, was found in a "middle"-class tomb among more than a hundred other objects. Three bronze kohl sticks, one in each tube, were also recovered. A craftsman shaped a solid block from local wood and then carved on one side the humorous detail of a playful monkey climbing. Next, he drilled three holes through the piece, carefully carving a neck around each aperture. Small ivory? pegs inserted in the front of each neck probably served as posts to attach covers for closing each tube's mouth. Two openings in the base are sealed with plaster; the third, with what is probably bitumen or pitch. A final smoothing of the tube's surface, perhaps supplemented with an application of oil, would have finished the container.

The ancient Egyptians exhibited their sense of humor in their literature and art. Numerous examples can be found in both religious and secular contexts. Puns and jests occur in stories and the rare religious myths, while many of the daily life scenes depicted on tomb walls present dialogue between ancient Egyptians that includes quips, sarcasm, and satirical comments. Both two- and three-dimensional art illustrate a wide variety of humorous representations including caricatures, political satire,

36

eroticism, and whimsical situations. The first three of these are found almost exclusively on ostraca (disposable fragments of stones and pottery) and papyrus, whereas the last is far more widespread.

The kohl tube depicted here is one example of a whimsical composition. In selecting a decorative element for the tube's exterior, the craftsman decided to illustrate a monkey scampering up the tube. By making the container from wood and in an upright style, the artisan played upon the primate's proclivity for climbing trees.

37.
Pomegranate-shaped Jar

(ceramic, paint)

Early Dynasty XVIII, reigns of Hatshepsut and Tuthmosis III
  (ca. 1479–1425 B.C.)
Abydos, D116
Height 13.6 cm; diameter 3 cm
ACC. 1917-490

Containers of pottery, faience, glass, and metal occasionally imitated the shapes of fruits and vegetables. The potter who formed this vessel chose a pomegranate for his model. The pomegranate was unknown in Egypt until early Dynasty XVIII, and the choice of its shape for this vessel may have reflected local interest in this newly available fruit. The pomegranate served as a food, a flavoring, and possibly a medicine. Its status as a prized fruit probably explains the following lines in a New Kingdom "love song": "Hearing your voice is pomegranate wine, I live by hearing it."[1]

This hand-formed jar from marl clay has a mouth shaped like the out-turned hull of the fruit at the point where the flower once bloomed. The vessel's body was lightly polished and the inside of the rim was painted red, probably imitating the flower's red-orange color. The jar's small size, very narrow neck and mouth, and its thorough polish suggest that it was designed to contain an expensive liquid that evaporated easily, such as perfume.

---

1. Pap. Harris 500 (II.c), trans. by M. Lichtheim, *Ancient Egyptian Literature*, vol. II: *The New Kingdom* (Berkeley: University of California Press, 1976), p. 192.

38.
Ex-Votos Dedicated to Hathor

a. Model Sistrum?	*b*. Plaque
(faience)	(bronze)
Deir el-Bahri	Deir el-Bahri
Mid to late Dynasty XVIII	Mid to late Dynasty XVIII
(ca. 1450–1295 B.C.)	(ca. 1450–1295 B.C.)
Length 3.7 cm; width 2.7 cm	Length 3.3. cm; width 2.1 cm
ACC. 2940-12b	ACC. 2940-14

When Pharaoh Hatshepsut (ca. 1479–1457 B.C.) built her mortuary temple at Deir el-Bahri, she included a small chapel dedicated to the goddess Hathor. Archaeological excavation at the site in 1904–05 brought to light many ex-votos left at the Hathor shrine by pious pilgrims. Ancient Egyptians who wanted to be remembered by a god or goddess would visit a shrine to leave these ex-votos, objects consecrated to a god or goddess, in hopes that they would honor the deity.

Ex-votos took a variety of forms. These pieces are examples of well-known types dedicated to Hathor. Figure 38a, only partially preserved, is probably a model sistrum, a rattle-like instrument sacred to this goddess. Her face forms the handle's upper section. The rest of the handle

38a

and rattle area above the face are now missing. The incised plaque, figure 38b, has an image of a cow, Hathor's animal form, with two amuletic eyes above its back. The plaque was pierced, perhaps so the offering could be suspended somewhere in the shrine.

Hathor was one of the oldest and most important goddesses in the Egyptian pantheon. Her primary associations were with the sky, fertility, music and dancing, and beauty. Often depicted as a woman with a crown composed of a solar disk supported by cow's horns, she also could appear as a cow or a woman with cow's ears. The bovine aspect of Hathor emphasized her importance as a mother goddess. On the chapel walls at Deir el-Bahri, reliefs depict a cow suckling Hatshepsut, thereby illustrating the goddess's role in nourishing the pharaoh when a child. Like other important cultic gods and goddesses, over time Hathor became part of the funerary ritual. Portrayed as a tree goddess titled "Lady of the Sycamore," Hathor offered sustenance to the dead.

39.
Double Kohl Tube

(ivory)

Early Dynasty XVIII, reigns of Hatshepsut and Tuthmosis III
(ca. 1479–1425 B.C.)
Abydos, D116
Height 8.1 cm; width 3.5 cm
ACC. 1917-10

Part of a large tomb group that belonged to an individual or individuals of the "middle" class, this kohl tube once contained crushed lead ore used as eye liner. The double-tube shape is a well-known New Kingdom style. The back

39

of this tube is flat while its front is tripartite, each side panel being angled. Two cylindrical necks with openings for the kohl sticks rise above the body of the piece. The tube is made from ivory, probably elephant ivory since it was popular and available in the New Kingdom.

By the end of the Old Kingdom, the Egyptians developed trade routes through Lower Nubia into Upper Nubia. By the New Kingdom, elephant ivory from the central African savanna was a common trade item. Elephant tusks are depicted in noblemen's tomb paintings as royal tribute from the Nubian territories. For the "middle" class, however, ivory was a luxury item and, therefore, not easily available. This tube, although not an elaborately made piece, was carefully repaired in antiquity. Someone took a small piece of ivory or bone and inserted it where the tube had lost a significant chunk. Then the side was filed to smooth the new surface flush with the original body. The restorer overestimated, however, resulting in a slight depression on the repaired side.

New Kingdom

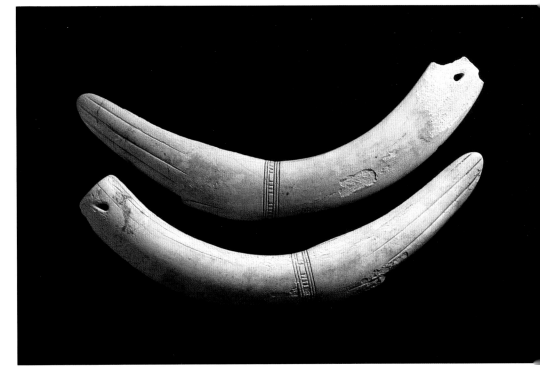

40.
Pair of Clappers

(ivory, paste)

Early Dynasty XVIII, reigns of Hatshepsut and Tuthmosis III
 (ca. 1479–1425 B.C.)
Abydos, D116
Length 25.2 cm; width 4.1 cm
ACC. 1917-8
Length 25.3 cm; width 3.9 cm
ACC. 1917-9

Music performed an important role in the private and public lives of the ancient Egyptians as a recreational pastime and a form of religious expression. Actual instruments have survived from burials, but even more are known from their illustrations on tomb and temple walls. The range of types is broad: rhythm makers, such as clappers, cymbals, drums, and tambourines; stringed instruments, including lutes, harps, and lyres; and woodwinds, principally flutes, clarinets, and oboes.

This pair of ivory clappers in the shape of two hands was used to keep time for dancers. Their graceful shape is enhanced by the craftsman's use of the curve in the tusk in forming the hands and wrist. Bracelets have been carved on each wrist and the incisions filled with black paste, causing the decoration to stand out against the white arms. At the end of each arm is a small hole through which a leather? thong was probably once threaded to hold the clappers together. The musician looped the thong around his or her wrist so that the clappers could not be easily dropped. These clappers were probably highly prized by their owner, since they are two of only four objects in ivory from a "middle"-class tomb containing over one hundred objects. Ivory would not have been easily available to this group of Egyptian society.

In the Old Kingdom (ca. 2750–2250 B.C.), the majority of musicians were men. In the New Kingdom, numerous depictions show that both men and women served as musicians, although never together in the same orchestra. Blind people are often shown playing musical instruments; the "blind harper" is a frequently encountered motif. Orchestras often performed at banquets as accompaniment to dancers or for the entertainment of the guests.

41.
Lid from a Canopic Jar
(ceramic, paint)

Early Dynasty XVIII, reigns of Hatshepsut and Tuthmosis III
 (ca. 1479–1425 B.C.)
Provenience unknown
Height 8.5 cm; diameter 10.5 cm
ACC. 2983-6980

This lid, which once capped a canopic jar, features a stylized male face wearing a striped headdress. The ancient potter fashioned the lid by first constructing by hand a conical cap. A mold containing the facial features was pressed into one side of the lid, after which the craftsman finished the details by hand. The artist used black paint to delineate the eyes, the wig's stripes, and the broad collar. Finally the piece was burnished, probably with a cloth, to give it a sealed surface and high polish.

Pottery was the most widely used material for containers, and many ancient Egyptians must have been prolific potters to accommodate the culture's requirements. As this piece shows, some workers were capable of achieving a high level of craftsmanship. Both written and pictorial records indicate that the ceramicists were men, although children and women may have assisted with such tasks as stoking the kilns and polishing or adding details to a vessel's surface.

The occupation was hot, dirty, and strenuous and, therefore, not a trade coveted by many ancient Egyptians. Anyone who had access to a multipurpose oven could make ceramics, although many communities must have set aside an area for pottery production, probably downwind from most of the settlement. Also, potters must have been among the craftsmen in workshops associated with temple, royal, and noble estates. Some everyday vessels were probably made by nonprofessional potters, possibly accounting for the variability in style and quality of certain types. Experienced potters manufactured the fancier containers, especially funerary items and mass-produced vessels needed by a village for local or export purposes. Certain types of containers, however, were made only in specific communities for distribution throughout Egypt. Decorated Ware vessels from the mid to late Predynastic Period (ca. 3650–3100 B.C.) and Blue Painted jars of late Dynasty XVIII (ca. 1390–1295 B.C.) represent two of these specialized wares.

42 a-h: Left to right, then front

43 a-g: Clockwise from top left

42.

Set of Cosmetic Vessels

(calcite)
Early Dynasty XVIII, reigns of Hatshepsut and Tuthmosis III
  (ca. 1479–1425 B.C.)
Abydos, D116

---

a. Shouldered Kohl Pot
Height 3.5 cm; diameter 3.7 cm
ACC. 1917-81

b. Small Cup
Height 5.6 cm; diameter 6 cm
ACC. 1917-89

c. Bag-shaped Jar
Height 5 cm; diameter 3.5 cm
ACC. 1917-88

d. Footed Jar with a Lid
Height 10 cm; diameter 5.6 cm
ACC. 1917-59 (lid)
ACC. 1917-87 (jar)

e. Shouldered Kohl Pot with a Lid
Height 7 cm; diameter 6 cm
ACC. 1917-85

f. Jar with a Pointed Base
Height 8.4 cm; diameter 4.2 cm
ACC. 1917-82

g. Shouldered Kohl Pot
Height 5.2 cm; diameter 5 cm
ACC. 1917-84

h. Shallow Bowl
Height 3.1 cm; diameter 8 cm
ACC. 1917-86

As early as the Neolithic Period (ca. 5450–3850 B.C.), the ancient Egyptians experimented with manufacturing stone containers. In the subsequent Naqada I Period (ca. 3850–3650 B.C.), stone vessels were still rare. A thousand years later, however, at the end of the Predynastic Period, artisans specializing in stone vessel carving had achieved an impressive level of skill.

The thousands of stone vessels from the royal tombs of Egypt's first three dynasties (ca. 3100–2675 B.C.) demonstrate a command of the abilities necessary for carving many varieties of rock, including calcite, basalt, slate, limestone, granite, and serpentine. During this period, the Egyptians used only stone and copper tools for carving and drilling and sandstone blocks, sand, and smooth stones for polishing. Craftsmen produced vessels in hard stone such as granite that were symmetrical and well polished. Those artisans who worked in softer stones, for example, slate, were capable of producing forms that illustrate a plasticity not often associated with stone.

Vessels of stone, especially calcite and serpentine, were common throughout the Pharaonic Period as small cosmetic containers. Many stone kohl pots (similar to figures 42e and g) and ointment jars (similar to figures 42c and

d) have been recovered from tombs. These calcite vessels, probably all associated with cosmetics in some way, were recovered from a "middle"-class tomb. Two kohl pots (figures 42e and g) still have evidence of the lead ore used as eye liner.

43.

Amulet Seals and Scarabs

---

a. Scarab
(faience)
Early Dynasty XVIII, reigns of
  Hatshepsut and Tuthmosis III
  (ca. 1539–1425 B.C.)
Abydos, D116
Length 1.5 cm; width 1.1 cm
ACC. 1917-78

b. Design Amulet with a
  Wedjet-eye Back
(faience)
Early Dynasty XVIII (ca. 1539–
  1425 B.C.)
Abydos, D64a
Length 1 cm; width 0.6 cm
ACC. 1917-328

c. Design Amulet in the Shape
  of a Goose
(glazed steatite)
Early Dynasty XVIII (ca. 1539–
  1425 B.C.)
Abydos, D111
Length 1.5 cm; width 0.9 cm
ACC. 1917-287

d. Plaque
(faience)
Early Dynasty XVIII, reigns of
  Hatshepsut and Tuthmosis III
  (ca. 1479–1425 B.C.)

Abydos, D116
Length 1.7 cm; width 1.3 cm
ACC. 1917-63

e. Plaque Bearing Tuthmosis III's
  Prenomen
(faience)
Early Dynasty XVIII, reign of
  Tuthmosis III (ca. 1479–
  1425 B.C.)
Abydos, D102
Length 1 cm; width 0.7 cm
ACC. 1917-206

f. Scarab Bearing Amun-Re's
  Name
(faience)
Mid-late Dynasty XVIII
  (ca. 1479–1295 B.C.)
Provenience unknown
Length 1.2 cm; width 0.9 cm
ACC. 1867-7b

g. Scarab with Hatshepsut's
  Prenomen
(faience)
Dynasty XVIII, reign of
  Hatshepsut (ca. 1479–
  1457 B.C.)
Abydos, D116
Length 1.4 cm; width 1.1 cm
ACC. 1917-60

The popularity of amulet seals and scarabs continued from the Middle Kingdom and Second Intermediate Period (see entry 23) into the subsequent New Kingdom. Their function remained the same, but stylistic details varied from their predecessors. Royal names remained potent protection (figures 43e and g), as did the scarab beetle (figure 43a). The overwhelming importance of the Theban god, Amun-Re, is reflected by the many design amulets and scarabs bearing his name (figure 43f). In

New Kingdom

addition to the traditional scarab back, there were other types of backs including amuletic signs (figure 43b) and animals (figure 43c). Plaques (figures 43d and e), which are design amulets with decorative elements on both sides, occur regularly.

44.
Head from a Nobleman's Statue

(diabase)

44

Mid Dynasty XVIII, reign of Tuthmosis IV (ca. 1400–1390 B.C.)
Deir el-Bahri
Height 20 cm; width 18 cm
ACC. 2940-3

During the field season of 1909–10, Edouard Naville recovered this fragment of a statue while excavating at Deir el-Bahri among the remains of the Dynasty XI temple. Although found in the debris of this temple, the head was once part of a nearly life-sized statue placed as a votive offering probably in the adjacent and better-known Dynasty XVIII temple belonging to Hatshepsut (ca. 1479–1457 B.C.). The elaborately styled wig and the quality of the craftsmanship proclaim its commission by an upper-class official. The thick arcing plastic eyebrows, the narrow eyes, the plump cheeks, and the roundness of the wig indicate that both the artisan and his subject worked during the reign of Tuthmosis IV.

Egypt, like any complex society, required that some people organize and regulate its other members. By Dynasty I (ca. 3100–2900 B.C.), ancient Egyptian inscriptions recorded titles of officials in a fully functioning government. Administrators were literate men possessing a knowledge of legal tradition. The official represented by this statue fragment was probably part of Egypt's government during the New Kingdom.

In the New Kingdom, the period from which Egyptologists have the most evidence, the government was divided into three major branches: the civil government, the royal domain, and the government of conquest regions. The civil government, the largest branch, regulated agriculture, collected taxes, administered justice, and kept civil order. Supervisors of the royal domain managed the king's personal assets. The last branch oversaw the foreign territories conquered by the army.

The king chose a few noblemen to fill key administrative positions including vizier,[1] overseer of the treasury,

and chief steward. These men, who reported directly to the pharaoh, provided strong centralized control. These same men were often linked to high religious and military positions by additional appointments. Stewards, mayors, and members of the local courts served as subordinate officials. Although minor bureaucrats passed their occupations on to their sons, the pharaoh appointed the highest officials. Women rarely possessed administrative positions, although examples are known.

Natural fracturing has occurred in this piece since its excavation as a result of the diabase's internal structure. This caused serious cracks throughout the piece, necessitating extensive conservation of the artifact.

1. During any reign, two viziers (for Upper and Lower Egypt) held the highest administrative office in the government. They reported directly to the pharaoh and were responsible for enforcing (royal) laws, appointing numerous civil servants, and supervising many governmental departments, especially those involved with the treasuries and taxation.

45.
Statue Fragment of a Scribe

(limestone)

Dynasty XVIII, reign of Amenhotep II (ca. 1427–1400 B.C.)
Deir el-Bahri
Height 16 cm; width 32 cm; depth 18 cm
ACC. 2940-1

This fragment represents the chest area from a statue that depicted a man seated with his legs crossed in the classic pose of a scribe at work. An ink palette, part of the hieroglyph that translates as "scribe," is inscribed with Amenhotep II's prenomen and rests on the statue's left

shoulder. The remainder of this glyph is carved in raised relief on the statue's back. Two hieroglyphs, *ankh (ꜥnḫ)* and *hetep (ḥtp)*, hang from a simple necklace. Although these hieroglyphs may be translated as a name, Ankh-hotep *(ꜥnḫ-ḥtp)*, Henry G. Fischer has suggested that they are most likely amuletic in nature, translating as "life" and "peace" or "May he live and be at peace."[1] A *wedjet*-eye and an uraeus surmounting a sun disk that are visible on the outer arm also have an amuletic function. Recovered by Edouard Naville during his excavations at Deir el-Bahri, this statue probably had been donated by its owner to the temple so that he could partake in the daily rites offered to the temple's gods.

Literacy was a highly prized skill that bestowed status on those who acquired it. Scribes were the only large group of people who could read, write, and calculate. Although Egyptologists know that upper-class women were educated and evidence suggests that some craftsmen could read if not write, the percentage of literacy in Egyptian society remained very low. The occupation of scribe was largely hereditary. Training started young and

lasted into the teens. In schools, students learned hieroglyphic and hieratic (cursive) scripts and mastered texts by recitation and copying. Scribes worked in temples, palaces, estates, towns, and the military. Highly competent men rose to eminent positions in government, while less-skilled scribes probably served the public.

The ancient Egyptians wrote a variety of texts. Among the literary forms were stories, instructions, hymns, poetry, biographies, and magical treatises. In addition, administrative documents including letters, business and legal records, and papyri concerning mathematics, medicine, and astronomy have been recovered.

This statue's high quality indicates the owner was upper class, an assumption supported by the rolls of fat, symbols of accumulated wealth, visible just below the chest. The nobleman who commissioned the statue probably chose to portray himself as a scribe because he was literate, not because he was a professional scribe. It is likely that he was a high-ranking government official.

---

1. Henry G. Fischer, "More Emblematic Uses from Ancient Egypt," *Metropolitan Museum Journal* 11 (1977): 125–28.

New Kingdom

46.

Shabti of Piaha

(limestone, paint)

Mid Dynasty XVIII (ca. 1479–1400 B.C.)
Abydos, Tomb of Djer
Height 18 cm; width 6.8 cm; thickness 3 cm
ACC. 1917-445

By the early Middle Kingdom (ca. 2025 B.C.), the site of Abydos had become permanently linked with the worship of Osiris, the ruler of the underworld. From the Middle Kingdom on, many ancient Egyptians visited the site as pilgrims, leaving offerings and erecting stelae, offering tables, and memorial chapels. They believed that their visits and gifts would bring them closer to Osiris after they died and they would be allowed to participate in the god's festivals and offerings. Wealthy people occasionally chose to leave shabtis, funerary statuettes (see entry 58), at certain places considered especially sacred, such as Abydos where Egypt's first pharaohs were buried. The tomb of Djer, the second king of Dynasty I, became one of these shrines at Abydos. We know from other

sources that Egyptians came to believe that Osiris was buried in Djer's tomb.

In 1900 while excavating Djer's tomb, Sir Flinders Petrie found this *shabti* whose inscriptions indicate that it belonged to Piaha *(pἰḥꝫ or pἰꝫḥꝫ)*. The *shabti* depicts a woman wearing a black wig decorated with two bands, one yellow and the other red, that probably imitate floral garlands. The face and jewelry retain red pigment; the incised hieroglyphs were painted black and the separation between registers, red. The statuette's style and quality indicate that it once belonged to an upper-class woman, although the only title that she had, "Lady of the House" *(nbt pr)*, is a very common one.

The overall shape of the *shabti*'s body indicates an early Dynasty XVIII date.[1] The elaborately curled wig, however, is unknown before the co-regency of Hatshepsut and Tuthmosis III, but was quite common from Tuthmosis IV on. The *shabti* cannot be later than the beginning of Tuthmosis IV's reign because it does not hold any implements. Therefore, the data suggest that a date encompassing the reigns of Tuthmosis III and Amenhotep II is probable.

1. I want to thank Donald Spanel, of The Brooklyn Museum, for his assistance in dating this piece.

47.

Stela Dedicated by Nebamen-Mennefer

(limestone, paint)

Mid Dynasty XVIII (ca. 1479–1390 B.C.)
Provenience unknown
Height 53.5 cm; width 34 cm; thickness 5.5 cm
ACC. 2983-99999a

The erecting of stelae, a tradition that flourished in the Middle Kingdom (ca. 2025–1627/1606 B.C.), remained in vogue in the early New Kingdom. Stelae could be dedicated to a variety of deities and were erected in the chapels associated with tombs or as votive offerings at temples. The stela represented here was dedicated to Osiris, Khentiamentiu, and Ptah-Sokar, all gods associated with the dead.

47. Detail

Stelae generally mention the name and titles of the donor and often identify other members of a family. This stela requests that offerings be given to the *ka* (spirit) of Nebamen-Mennefer *(imn-nb mn-nfr)*.[1] Nebamen-Mennefer is the man in the upper right offering liquid from a vase to a seated man and woman who are most likely his parents. Nebamen-Mennefer bears the titles "Child of the Kap" *(ḥrd n kȝp)*, "Overseer of the Numerous Megau People of His Majesty and Children of the Kep" *(ḥry mgȝw ʿȝ n ḥm.[f] ḥrd.w m kȝp)*, and "Chief of the Great River" *(ḥȝ.ty-ʿ n itrw ʿȝ)*. These titles suggest that his responsibilities included serving as a page and supervising a group of young Nubian soldiers belonging to the king. The meaning of "Chief of the Great River" is less clear, but perhaps Nebamen-Mennefer was responsible for a local canal or a branch of the Nile River in the Delta.

The upper left part of the stela has been broken so that the head of the seated woman is gone. The inscription in the five registers below the scene informs us that Henout *(ḥnwt)* was the mother of Nebamen-Mennefer, probably supplying the missing name of the woman in the upper register.

A stela in the Musée Calvert in Avignon, France,[2] provides possible identification for Nebamen-Mennefer's parents. That stela was also dedicated by a Nebamen-Mennefer who bears very similar titles to those on our stela. The Avignon stela also mentions his parents; his mother's name, Henouti-hemi, is a longer version of the Carnegie name. In addition, the hieroglyphs that compose the father's name, Paaha *(pȝ-ʿḥȝ),* on the Avignon

piece match the remnants of signs visible on the Carnegie stela, indicating that both stelae represent the same family.

In the latter part of Dynasty XVIII, Pharaoh Akhenaten (ca. 1352–1336 B.C.) shifted the focus of state religion in ancient Egypt away from the traditional New Kingdom god, Amun-Re, to his favorite deity, the Aten. Along with the forced closing of all temples not dedicated to Aten, the name of Amun-Re was obliterated from many inscriptions dedicated to him. Some of the damage on this stela reflects this religious fervor of Akhenaten's reign. Nebamen-Mennefer's name contains the name of god, Amun. Therefore, the "Amun" in Nebamen-Mennefer's name was erased in both places where it was inscribed. Additionally, the overzealous desecrator probably mistook the meaning of a hieroglyph in "Mennefer," destroying that one as well.

---

1. I have chosen to read his name as Nebamen-Mennefer, but it is equally possible to read it as Amenneb-Mennefer.

2. I want to thank Paul O'Rourke, Department of Egyptian Art, The Brooklyn Museum, for bringing the stela in Avignon (Inv. 1) to my attention and assisting with the translation of several of the names and titles on our stela.

48.
Block Statue

(limestone)

Dynasty XVIII (ca. 1539–1295 B.C.)
Deir el-Bahri
Height 21.5 cm; width 15 cm; depth 17.5 cm
ACC. 2940-2a

The dedication of stelae and statues as votive offerings to the god or goddess of a temple was an accepted way of ensuring the goodwill of that deity. The so-called block statue, whose origin was in the early Middle Kingdom, was a popular sculptural type through the Late Period (ca. 664–332 B.C.). Block statues depict a man seated on the ground with his knees drawn up to his chest and his arms folded across the knees. This stance provides a basic cubic structure, a form which is enhanced when the individual wears an enveloping ankle-length cloak, such as in the Carnegie piece. Egyptologists do not agree on why the ancient Egyptians chose this form for statuary, but the style certainly provided a large, flat area suitable for an inscription.

This statue, unfortunately missing its head, exemplifies block statues from Dynasty XVIII (ca. 1539–1295 B.C.). Here, the man's cloak has enveloped all but the hands, located on top of the statue in front of his missing head: one of the hands is clenched while the other lies flat. The inscription running across the lower legs and around the base reveals an offering formula dedicated to Amun-Re and Hathor by Amenhotep (*ỉmn-ḥtp*), a man whose titles are "Rewarded by the King" (*ḥsy n nswt*), "Favorite" (*ỉmy-ỉb*), and "Chamberlain" (*ỉmy-ḫnt*).

49.
Relief Fragment with a Portion of the Aten Disk

(limestone, paint)

Dynasty XVIII, reign of Akhenaten (ca. 1352–1336 B.C.)
El-Amarna, Maru-aten temple
Length 14.5 cm; width 13.2 cm
ACC. 7043-8

During the first half of Dynasty XVIII (ca. 1539–1400 B.C.), Amun-Re became the most prominent god in the ancient Egyptian pantheon and his main temple, located near the modern village of Karnak, was greatly expanded. In the latter half of Dynasty XVIII (ca. 1352 B.C.), Amenhotep IV (Akhenaten) chose to break with the Egyptian religious tradition dominated by Amun-Re by elevating the Aten disk, an obscure manifestation of the sun god, to an unprecedented level. In the fifth year of his reign, except for the king and his wife, Nefertiti, who played an important part in the cult, the other gods ceased to be recognized and their temples were closed.

Initially Amenhotep IV ruled from Thebes, where he continued a building program centered at Karnak but his emphasis was on Aten. In his fifth year, he moved to a

48

49

50

50.
Canopic Jar Lid

(calcite, paste, paint)

Late Dynasty XVIII, reign of Horemheb (ca. 1323–1295 B.C.)
Provenience unknown
Height 15.5 cm; diameter 15 cm
ACC. 9007-18

This lid was once part of a set of canopic jars destined to hold the internal organs of a member of ancient Egypt's upper class. The modeling of the eyes and eyelids, the slight smile, and the triangular shape of the face suggest the head dates to the reign of Horemheb, the last king of Dynasty XVIII (ca. 1323–1295 B.C.). Although neither the owner's name nor title survives, the piece's quality indicates that he was a wealthy man. The elaborate headdress and styled beard suggest the lid's owner possessed a high rank as well.

Ancient Egyptian society was structured into broad social classes with well-established, but not inflexible, boundaries. The pharaoh and his immediate family possessed the highest rank by their birth. They had frequent contact with the nobility, which included secondary branches of the royal house and high-ranking nonroyal families. Children of noblemen often attended school with royal offspring, and the pharaoh selected his most important officials from among the upper class.

Minor officials, including some scribes, priests, and "judges," belonged to "middle"-class families sometimes of provincial origin. Also, certain highly skilled craftsmen and probably merchants could be included in the "middle" class. Members of the nobility and "middle" class often acquired titles, sometimes indicating occupation but often identifying rank, that is, social status. The peasantry, including farmers, hunters, fishermen, servants, and certain artisans, composed the lower class, the largest group of ancient Egyptians. The lowest-ranking members of Egyptian society were the slaves, nonfree people brought to Egypt after their homeland's conquest.

Both birth and occupation were used to determine an Egyptian's social status. Social mobility was possible, however, especially within the military or through education. Records also indicate the occasional emancipation of slaves, which allowed them to move into other social classes. Social status cut across some occupations. For example, the priesthood, the military, and the bureaucracy each contained members of several classes.

virgin site and built a new royal city, Akhetaten (el-Amarna). The city included private and official or administrative palaces, numerous temples and chapels, and several residential zones that provided housing for all the urban inhabitants. Officials had spacious houses; the workmen's quarters were more crowded.

Among the temples at el-Amarna constructed for Aten's veneration, the Great Temple for the Aten is the best known. Akhenaten, however, also built a vast complex called Maru-aten in the southern section of the city. It comprised a large walled enclosure whose open expanse was broken by gardens, carefully laid-out pools, and small open-air pavilions. Although its exact use is debated, most Egyptologists feel that the Maru-aten was a cultic structure used by the god Aten in the same manner that we use a garden.

The excavation report of C. Leonard Woolley's 1921 field season at el-Amarna indicates that this fragment probably came from the Maru-aten, most likely from the small temple (Building II) in the eastern part of the precinct. The fragment displays a partial representation of the sun disk, Aten (see the line drawing for a completed version). To the disk's left, the word most commonly translated as "horizon" (_ȝḫt_) is visible. The small size of this piece exemplifies the thorough destruction carried out on the structures at el-Amarna by Pharaoh Horemheb (ca. 1323–1295 B.C.) while he was returning Egypt to its cultural traditions.

51.
Dovetail or Cramp

(wood)

Dynasty XIX, reign of Sety I (ca. 1294–1279 B.C.)
Provenience unknown
Length 21.6 cm; width 9.5 cm
ACC. 2147-8

Nearly thirty-three hundred years ago, this dovetail held in position two large stone blocks in a building constructed by the order of Pharaoh Sety I. His cartouche is clearly incised on the top, the cramp's only finished side. The ends and remaining sides still exhibit the marks of adzes used in the manufacturing process.

Several building materials were available to the Egyptians. The archaeological evidence suggests the earliest structures were short-term dwellings of wattle and daub (straw or grass woven together and plastered with mud). The earliest-known structures of mud brick are tombs from the Naqada II Period (ca. 3650–3300 B.C.). Mud brick was the building material for houses and palaces throughout Pharaonic history and often enclosed the graves of "middle"-class people. An ample supply of mud and straw was available in the Nile Valley, making mud brick an inexpensive building material. The almost total absence of rainfall made mud brick well suited to the climate.

The development and spread of copper tools in the late Predynastic Period (ca. 3100 B.C.) allowed for the introduction of a new building medium, stone. From the earliest blocks of granite and limestone in tombs from Dynasty I (ca. 3100–2900 B.C.) to the final Pharaonic style buildings of Trajan and Hadrian (A.D. 98–138), the Egyptians constructed their monumental temples, colossal statues, and royal and upper-class tombs most often in stone. The methods for quarrying and carving the massive blocks of limestone, sandstone, and granite depended solely on time and manpower. Laborers in the quarry first used stone pounders and copper tools to separate most of a block from the surrounding stone matrix and then employed wooden wedges, swelled by water, to force its final separation. The workers moved the blocks from the quarry on wooden sledges, easing them along by pouring water along the ground. At the river, large barges were loaded with the blocks that were then towed to the building site. Craftsmen dressed the stone using wooden mallets and stone and copper tools of several sizes. Final polishing was done with finely ground sand and possibly smooth pebbles.

The men who undertook the final dressing and polishing were artisans, but the large numbers of unskilled workers required during the stages of quarrying and transporting were assembled from a number of sources. Criminals and prisoners of war were sent to work in quarries or mines, while peasants were enrolled into short-term, compulsory labor levies as a form of taxation.

New Kingdom

52.
Hoe
(wood)

Dynasty XIX–XX (ca. 1295–1070 B.C.)
Deir el-Bahri
Handle: length 38.8 cm; width 5 cm
ACC. 2940-6
Blade: length 34.5 cm; width 14.5 cm
ACC. 2940-6a

Agriculture in ancient Egypt required only a few basic tools: plows, hoes, baskets, sickles, forks, and scoops. Hoes such as this one were used in breaking dirt clods formed during plowing and for tending the growing crops. The ancient Egyptians also used hoes to move dirt during building or brick making. This hoe is made from two pieces, a handle and a blade, that were fitted together and then bound with rope. The binding of modern rope that now holds both parts together is based on original attachments known from other hoes. The object does not show signs of heavy use. Its excavation at Deir el-Bahri and its lack of wear patterns suggest that this hoe was used to mix water and dirt for mud brick.

Egyptologists do not know much about farmers' lives beyond their daily tasks in the fields. As members of the lower class, full-time farmers were illiterate and, therefore, did not have the education or income to leave behind their personal histories. Farmers endured a hard but secure life, since serious deprivation appears to have been an uncommon circumstance. All farming was done by hand with the occasional use of cattle to pull plows. On small private farms, most family members were in-

volved in agricultural activities; women are seen in tomb paintings gleaning the fields during harvest. A large number of farmers, however, worked on estates owned by others and were paid in food and clothing. Some farmers rented land from wealthier people, giving a portion of the harvest in payment to the leaser.

It appears likely that most of Egypt's adult male population spent some time farming. Although there were full-time farmers, during and immediately following inundation most men were drafted through corvée (forced labor by the government as taxation) to increase the personnel available for dredging irrigation canals, surveying land boundaries, and preparing the ground for planting. Avoidance of corvée carried stiff penalties for the individual and sometimes his family. Noblemen and scribes, the literate upper class, were the only people consistently excluded from the corvée. Most noblemen were automatically involved in the agricultural system, however, because they owned farms and supervised royal or temple agricultural land.

53.
Lid of a
Canopic Jar
(wood)

Dynasty XIX–XX (ca. 1295–1070 B.C.)
Provenience unknown
Height 14.5 cm; diameter 14 cm
ACC. 21538-6

We know that the ancient artisan fashioned this canopic jar lid representing a male face from the central portion of a log since the tree's pith and surrounding heartwood are clearly visible on the lid's base. The jar itself is missing so there is no record of its original owner, whose name might have been inscribed on its base.

Wood was a popular material among ancient Egyptian craftsmen for large objects such as boats, chariots, beds, shrines, and coffins, as well as for smaller items such as statues, boxes, *shabti*s, canopic jars, cosmetic equipment, tools, and inlays. The craftsmen's skills can be seen in the close-fitting joints on large objects and the finely carved decorations on small items. Usable Egyptian timber was uncommon and only a few types of local trees were used. The tamarisk, sycamore fig, and acacia provided wood dense enough to work, while the date palm yielded planks usable in roof construction. For high-quality wood, often found in the construction of coffins and boats, the Egyptians looked abroad. Ancient records name many types of wood, but few have been correlated with known species of trees. Cedar (from Syro-Palestine) and ebony (imported via Nubia) are two woods that remained common trade items throughout much of Egyptian history.

54.
Funerary Pectoral Depicting Re-Horakhty

(steatite)

Dynasty XIX–XX (ca. 1295–1070 B.C.)
Probably Thebes
Length 8.5 cm; width 11 cm; thickness 1.4 cm
ACC. 11983-15

The period immediately following the Opening-of-the-Mouth ceremony, when the mummy was brought to life, was exceedingly dangerous for the deceased. Therefore, each individual, according to his or her social position and wealth, arranged for protective inscriptions and symbols to be placed on his or her mummy or in the

54

tomb. Protection took many forms, all of which were intended to secure for the deceased a safe journey to the underworld and the type of afterlife that all Egyptians envisioned.

This pectoral was designed to ensure that a man named Amenhotep *(imn-ḥtp)* would join Re on his daily voyage across the sky. Therefore, it probably was placed on the chest of Amenhotep's mummy as a piece of funerary jewelry. The pectoral depicts Re in his falcon-headed aspect, Re-Horakhty. He stands under a shrine on the deck of his solar barque, which as Re-Horakhty he used daily to sail across the heavens. He is accompanied by a phoenix, a bird the ancient Egyptians believed represented the *ba* (spirit) of Re.

The inscription on the pectoral's back face dedicates the piece to "Osiris, lord of Abydos." The owner, Amenhotep, bore several titles which together indicate that he was a full-time priest. He was a *"Wab* Priest in the Front for the Cult of Amun" *(wꜥb ḥ3.t n imn)* and *"Wab* Priest in the Front for the Cult of Mut" *(wꜥb ḥ3.t n mwt),* Amun-Re's consort. Thus when the sacred barque was carried in a procession, Amenhotep was in front of the other priests. His most important title, however, was "Prophet of the Hearts of [King] Amenhotep" *(ḥm-nṯr p3 ib-ib n imn-ḥtp).* As such, he was the priest of a cult statue dedicated to the worship of Amenhotep, most likely in a cult temple of Amenhotep I. The inscription also records the name of Amenhotep's father, Horsaast *(ḥr-s3-3st),* and states that he too was a *"Wab* Priest in the Front for the Cult of Mut." It appears likely that Amenhotep inherited one of his priestly positions from his father.

The Nationalmuseet in Copenhagen, Denmark, has in its collection a pectoral of similar size and material that illustrates a scarab beetle on a solar barque (no. 8189). The inscription almost duplicates The Carnegie's piece although some of the titles have been shortened and his father's name (but not the title) eliminated. Since the scarab beetle represents Re in his morning aspect and The Carnegie's piece depicts Re during the day, it seems reasonable to hypothesize that at one time there was a third pectoral whose composition portrayed Re as Atum, the afternoon or setting sun, thereby completing a set of pectorals symbolizing all the aspects of the sun god, Re.

Unframed pectorals are rare and so the overall shape is currently undatable. Nevertheless, a date of the Ramesside Period (Dynasty XIX–XX, ca. 1295–1070 B.C.) has been assigned to this piece based on inscriptional and iconographic data. The general style of the figures, however, is consistent with a late New Kingdom date. The

depiction of either Re-Horakhty or the phoenix on a solar barque in Theban tomb paintings is very common during Dynasty XIX and XX. For instance, in Sennedjem's tomb at Deir el-Medina, dated to Dynasty XIX, a phoenix appears beside Re-Horakhty. Although Amenhotep is a very common name throughout the New Kingdom, his father's name, Horsaast, is rare before the late New Kingdom. These points suggest the Ramesside Period date. The three cults named in Amenhotep's titles also were very important during the late New Kingdom.

55.
Coffin of Heramenpenaf

(gessoed cedar, paint)

Late Dynasty XX, reign of Ramesses XI–early Third Intermediate
  Period (ca. 1099–1070/69 B.C.)
Provenience unknown
Lid and base: length 198 cm.; width 50 cm; height 50.5 cm
ACC. 22266-3b (lid)
ACC. 22266-3c (inner lid)
ACC. 22266-3d (base)

Ancient Egyptians believed that one of the requirements for a successful afterlife was the preservation of the body, which would serve as the home of the deceased's *ka* (spirit). Thus, the bodies of most Egyptians were subjected to some form of mummification and then placed in coffins which were left in tombs for eternal protection.

This anthropoid coffin consists of three pieces: a base, a lid, and an inner lid which was laid directly upon the mummy. The exterior is embellished with scenes and offering formulae commonly found on coffins of the late New Kingdom and Third Intermediate Period (ca. 1295–653 B.C.); these include the deceased making an offering to Osiris; the triad of Nut, Geb, and Shu; and Nephthys and Isis mourning Osiris. The interior lacks decoration. The entire coffin exhibits hack marks made by axes or adzes. The deceased's face on both lids and the hands on the outer lid are missing. Perhaps they were once gilded and robbers chopped them off for the gold.

Inscriptions down the center of the two lids and on the base identify the coffin's owner as Heramenpenaf *(ḥr-imn-pnꜥ.f),* "Administrator of the Tomb" *(d3r n p3 ḥr)* and "Wab Priest for the Cult of Amenhotep I" *(wꜥb ḏsr-k3-rꜥ imn-ḥtp).* To conserve space, the scribe omitted certain hieroglyphs in Heramenpenaf's name. However, his com-

plete name and the title "Administrator of the Tomb" are distinctive and match an individual mentioned in letters from the tenth year of the "Renaissance," a period largely contained within the reign of Ramesses XI (ca. 1099–1070/1069 B.C.). "Administrator of the Tomb" was a title applied to supervisors involved with work in what today is called the Valley of the Kings. Heramenpenaf probably was responsible for supervising workmen laboring on Ramesses XI's tomb.

His second title indicates that he served as a minor priest at a temple of Amenhotep I, a deified pharaoh whose cult had a large following at Deir el-Medina, the village of workmen building the royal tombs. Heramenpenaf may well have lived in this town, although his tomb has not been identified there. If he lived into the beginning of Dynasty XXI (ca. 1070) and after the village's abandonment, he may have been buried somewhere in the Theban necropolis in a tomb not yet discovered.

The inner lid presents the deceased in the same position as on the coffin lid, but with a different decorative scheme that illustrates several common types of funerary jewelry. The close-up of the inner lid shows examples of this jewelry on the deceased's chest. Above Heramenpenaf's crossed arms, a pectoral of a winged scarab symbolizes rebirth. Beaded bracelets encircle his wrists. Below his hands, a rectangular pectoral displays two winged uraei (aroused cobras) flanking another scarab beetle.

The coffin contained the remains of a poorly preserved mummy. Heavy damage, possibly inflicted by the same people responsible for the coffin's condition, has resulted in a shattered mummy. X-rays[1] of the mummy revealed an adult male, but the skeleton's fragmentary state prevented identifying the man's age at death or any medical problems he had.

55. Detail

1. The radiographic studies on this and other Carnegie mummies (see entries 60, 76, 80, and 82) were made possible through the generosity of Forbes Metropolitan Health Center, Pittsburgh, Pennsylvania. Dr. Joseph A. Marasco, Jr., Chairman of Radiology, directed the work with able assistance from members of his department.

New Kingdom

The two female faces wearing an oversized crosshatched wig were made from the same mold. Below each face, two arms are brought together over the breasts. An almost identical vase made of sheet gold is in the Petrie Museum, University College, London. Although female faces are often identified as Hathor, Gretchen L. Spalinger suggests that there is no reason to identify this image as such; a simple female identification is more accurate.[1] The vase's small size and dense material suggest it was designed to contain a precious or volatile substance such as oil, unguent, or perfume.

1. G.L. Spalinger, "Catalog No. 113," in *Egypt's Golden Age*, eds. E. Brovarski, S. Doll, and R. Freed (Boston: The Museum of Fine Arts, 1982), pp. 124–25.

56.
Jar with Two Faces
(faience)

New Kingdom (ca. 1539–1070 B.C.)?
Provenience unknown
Height 10.6 cm; diameter 2 cm
ACC. 9007-52

Although vases bearing representations of deities or humans were never common in ancient Egypt, archaeologists have recovered a variety of types. This faience jar with two female images was made in stages. The body was fashioned in two halves and then imprecisely joined. The jar's neck was hand modeled separately and attached to the body. In addition, two small unpierced lugs were added on the vessel's shoulder between the two images. The final form was glazed. Now most of the glaze is missing, although small remnants persist in the crevices of the wigs and faces.

57.
Military Equipment

a. Axhead (bronze) Early Dynasty XVIII, reigns of Hatshepsut and Tuthmosis III (ca. 1539–1425 B.C.) Abydos, D116 Length 14 cm; width 10 cm ACC. 1917-12	*d.* Arrowhead (bronze) Early Dynasty XVIII (ca. 1539–1425 B.C.) Abydos, D64a Length 5.6 cm; width 1 cm ACC. 1917-324
b. Spearhead (bronze) Third Intermediate Period (ca. 1070–653 B.C.) Abydos, D98 Length 9.8 cm; width 1.7 cm ACC. 1917-265	*e.* Axhead (bronze) First Intermediate Period– Middle Kingdom (ca. 2250–1627/1606 B.C.) Provenience unknown Length 11 cm; width 11.5 cm ACC. 9074-2254
c. Arrowhead (bronze) Third Intermediate Period (ca. 1070–653 B.C.) Abydos, D98 Length 7.7 cm; width 1.2 cm ACC. 1917-264	*f.* Dagger Handle (wood) New Kingdom? (ca. 1539–1070 B.C.) Provenience unknown Height 12.2 cm; width 6 cm ACC. 9074-2464

Although this equipment belongs to different chronological periods, the assemblage represents some weapon types available to New Kingdom soldiers. The axheads (figures 57a and e), the spearhead (figure 57b), the arrowheads (figures 57c and d) and the dagger handle (figure 57f) all could have been used by foot soldiers,

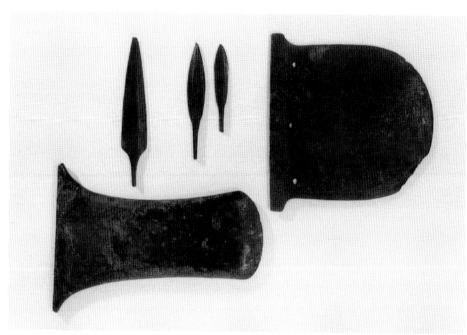

57a-e: Left to right

57f

although charioteers also used the bow and arrow as their weapon. The New Kingdom army consisted of companies of foot soldiers, an elite core of charioteers, and men who were assigned to naval vessels, as well as civil officials such as scribes.

The army included career soldiers in addition to conscripted individuals and, from the late New Kingdom on (ca. 1185–332 B.C.), mercenaries in growing numbers. Children often spent their early years as servants in the barracks while apprenticing as a soldier. A successful military career could launch an ambitious man into a more lucrative assignment in the government. The highest position, general, was given to the crown prince or to men from upper-class families. Noblemen of this rank, occasionally through marriage, supplied the royal house with new blood. Tuthmosis I, Horemheb, and Ramesses I, for example, were all generals chosen to be pharaoh when the reigning king had no heirs.

During peacetime, the standing army garrisoned the palaces and the fortresses on Egypt's borders and in its territories. Reserves, generally farmers, remained available for wartime demand. In addition to supplying the garrisons, soldiers were also used as expeditionary forces for trading or mining operations and were assigned to public ceremonies that required large numbers of men.

The dagger handle (figure 57f) is especially interesting, although the blade is missing. The upper portion of the handle is divided into two parts, each depicting a falcon's head. These may have symbolized the pharaoh, who was the titular head of Egypt's military force, or the god Horus, who was the traditional ruler of all Egypt. The doubled-headed motif probably represented the country's traditional duality. Carved in the handle's center is a schematic image composed of two eyes, a nose, and a mouth. This face represents a generalization of an Egyptian enemy. Its placement on the hilt allowed the owner, when drawing the blade, to crush symbolically Egypt's enemies.

New Kingdom

Third Intermediate Period, CIRCA 1070–653 B.C.

and

Late Period, CIRCA 664–332 B.C.

Third Intermediate Period

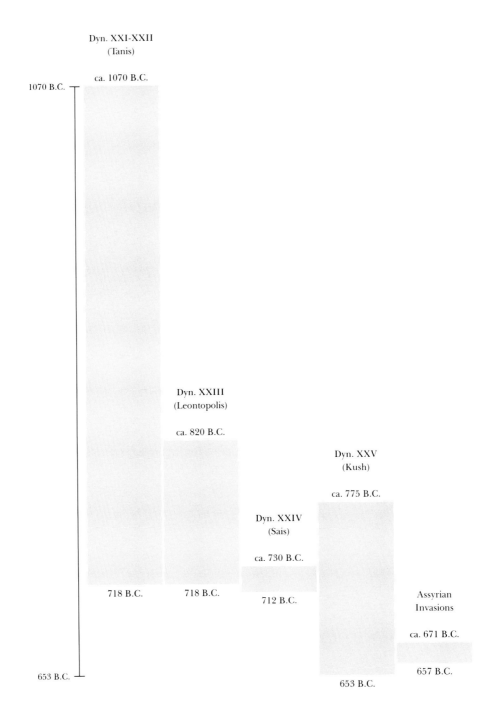

Dyn. XXI-XXII
(Tanis)

ca. 1070 B.C.

1070 B.C.

Dyn. XXIII
(Leontopolis)

ca. 820 B.C.

Dyn. XXV
(Kush)

ca. 775 B.C.

Dyn. XXIV
(Sais)

ca. 730 B.C.

718 B.C.   718 B.C.

712 B.C.

Assyrian
Invasions

ca. 671 B.C.

657 B.C.

653 B.C.

653 B.C.

Note: A location in parentheses indicates the seat of that dynasty's ruling family.

INTRODUCTION

The Third Intermediate Period (Dynasty XXI–XXV, ca 1070–653 B.C.) was characterized by continuous low-scale conflict throughout Egypt that often resulted in concomitant dynasties ruling from different parts of the country. That there were different kings ruling similtaneously makes the history of this period extremely complex and often confusing. During this period, military might, not royal authority, dictated successful rule. In Dynasty XXI (ca. 1070–945 B.C.), the royal family resided in Tanis, a Delta city, while the High Priest of Amun, now the most powerful government position, ruled Upper Egypt from Thebes, controlling most of the country's wealth and power.

Although Ramesses III had repeatedly fought the Libyans during his reign, by the late New Kingdom many Libyans had infiltrated the Delta, settling in certain provinces. By about 820 B.C., power shifted from the royal family in Tanis (Dynasty XXI continuing through Dynasty XXII, ca. 1070–718 B.C.) to a series of Libyan kings in Leontopolis (Dynasty XXIII, ca. 820–718 B.C.). These kings were better able to rule part of Upper Egypt because they acquired control over the office of High Priest of Amun at Thebes. But toward the end of Dynasty XXIII, these kings were no longer strong enough to hold the entire country and they vied for control with the rulers at Sais (Dynasty XXIV, ca. 730–712 B.C.) and the kings from Nubian Kush who made up Dynasty XXV (ca. 775–653 B.C.). Eventually the Kushite kings, especially Taharqa, controlled much of Egypt's resources and championed a revival in Egyptian cultural, religious, and literary traditions.

Assyrians occupied Egypt sporadically between 671 and 657 B.C., but problems at home eventually caused them to abandon it. Petty native Egyptian rulers under the Assyrians at Sais quickly stepped in to fill the void,

thus beginning Dynasty XXVI (ca. 664–525 B.C.). Psamtik I, the first true king of the Late Period (Dynasty XXVI–XXXI, ca. 664–332 B.C.) used military might to reunify Egypt. He stabilized the economy through international trade, especially with Greece and Phoenicia, resulting in the settlement of Greek mercenaries in the Delta. The Dynasty XXVI kings sought to revitalize ancient Egyptian tradition inspired by the Old Kingdom monuments, thereby producing a reemergence of native Egyptian culture.

Pharaoh Ahmose II (Amasis) increased Egypt's wealth and undertook a building program, but his successor was unable to ward off the Persians, and Egypt fell prey to that empire's expansionist policies. The Egyptians resented the Persians (Dynasty XXVII, ca. 525–404/401 B.C.), who used Egypt solely as a source of income for the Persian empire, draining temple incomes. As a distant outpost, however, Egypt was difficult to control and the Persians lost Egypt to the last native pharaohs (Dynasty XXIX–XXX, ca. 399–342 B.C.). The Persians briefly regained Egypt during Dynasty XXXI before losing their entire empire, including Egypt, to Alexander the Great (ca. 332 B.C.).

58.

Shabtis

58a–i: Left to right

a. Shabti
(wood, paint)
Dynasty XVII (ca. 1627/1606–
  1539 B.C.)
Abydos
Height 13.2 cm; width 3.2 cm
ACC. 1662-6

b. Shabti with Illegible Name
(gessoed wood)
Dynasty XIX–XX (ca. 1295–
  1070 B.C.)
Provenience unknown
Height 17.5 cm; width 4.4 cm
ACC. 2983-6653

c. Shabti of "Lady of the House"
  Nuast?
(ceramic, paint)

Dynasty XIX–XX (ca. 1295–
  1070 B.C.)
Abydos
Height 13.6 cm; width 4.2 cm
ACC. 1662-10

d. Shabti
(limestone)
Dynasty XIX–XX (ca. 1295–
  1070 B.C.)
Provenience unknown
Height 18.5 cm; width 4.9 cm
ACC. 2983-6768

e. Shabti of "Overseer of the
  Treasury" Pahermer?
(faience)

Dynasty XIX–XX (ca. 1295–
  1070 B.C.)
Abydos
Height 12.4 cm; width 3.9 cm
ACC. 1662-2

f and g. Unnamed *Shabti*s
(ceramic, paint)
Third Intermediate Period
  (ca. 1070–653 B.C.)
Provenience unknown
Height 6.4 cm; width 2 cm
ACC. 2983-6646
Height 6.4 cm; width 1.7 cm
ACC. 2983-6747

h. Shabti of "Prophet of Amun"
  Nesankhefenmaat?

(faience)
Third Intermediate Period
  (ca. 1070–653 B.C.)
Abydos
Height 15.6 cm; width 4.3 cm
ACC. 1662-7

i. Shabti
(faience)
Late Period (ca. 664–332 B.C.)
Provenience unknown
Height 17.7 cm; width 4.6 cm
ACC. 2983-6751

During Dynasty XI (ca. 2025–1979 B.C.), a new type of funerary object appeared in tombs: small statues in the form of nude humans, often wrapped in linen and placed in model coffins. They were inscribed with a prayer for food offerings, although they probably also functioned as an alternative abode for the *ka* (a person's vital force). By the Middle Kingdom (ca. 2025–1627/1606 B.C.), the figures had become mummiform in shape and their inscriptions clearly join the deceased with Osiris, the god of the underworld, who rose to prominence during this period. By late Dynasty XII (ca. 1850 B.C.), the statuettes' original function as a residence for the *ka* had expanded greatly. Although the original identification with the tomb owner was never lost, the figures were seen primarily as

workers who performed a service for the deceased, and they became known by the ancient Egyptians as *shabti*s. Rapidly *shabti*-figures came to represent the deceased's servants in the afterlife and were so popular that they replaced the model servant statues previously deposited in upper-class graves of the Old and Middle Kingdoms (ca. 2750–1627/1606 B.C.). As their purpose changed so did their name, first to *shawabti*, then to *ushabti*. The latter may be translated as "Answerer," a reference to the statues' status as servants.

From the New Kingdom through the Ptolemaic Period (from ca. 1539–30 B.C.), *shabti*s toiled as farmers in the afterlife. *Shabti*s often carry hoes, seed bags, picks, and water pots, reflecting their farming activities. Since most

59

Egyptians were subjected to corvée (forced labor as a form
of taxation), they purchased *shabti*s to be their substitutes
when Osiris called upon them to farm the eternal fields.
For the ancient Egyptians, the exchange of one individual for another to perform required work was an acceptable practice. Interestingly, there are *shabti*s that are inscribed for royalty and nobility, men and women who were
not involved in the corvée, implying that these people
were not excused from labor in the afterlife. It has been
suggested that from the Third Intermediate Period on
*shabti*s no longer were substitutes for the deceased but
similar to personal slaves.

By the late New Kingdom (ca. 1185 B.C.), a well-
equipped tomb had 365 *shabti*-figures, one for every day
of the year, and 36 overseers carrying whips (figure 58g)
to make sure the work was done. Records indicate that
people bought *shabti*s from temple workshops. The *shabti*s
are often inscribed with the owner's name and titles and
sometimes record Chapter 6 of the "Book of the Dead."

Over their long history, *shabti*s varied a great deal in
style reflecting changing functions and fashion. They were
made from a variety of materials, but faience, limestone,
and painted wood or clay were the most popular. Figure
58a, the earliest in this group, is a peg-like figure representative of *shabti*s of Dynasty XVII (ca. 1627/1606–1539
B.C.).

59.
Lintel from a Building

(limestone, paint)

Dynasty XXI, reign of Siamen (ca. 979–960 B.C.)
Memphis
Length 99.8 cm; width 60.2 cm; thickness (at widest part) 23.1 cm
ACC. 3755-1a

This piece is half of a stone lintel from a mud-brick building commissioned by the little-known Pharaoh Siamen.
Excavated by Sir Flinders Petrie in 1908 at Memphis, the
most important capital of ancient Egypt, the Carnegie
lintel was one of several that marked the building's en-
trances. The kneeling figure represents a priest who holds
his left hand up in adoration of Pharaoh Siamen, represented only by his names inscribed before the priest; in
his right hand, the priest grips an ostrich feather fan.
The hieroglyphs identify him as Ankhefenmut (*ᶜnḫ.f-n-
mwt*), the son of Hatiay (*ḥꜣ.t-iꜣy*). Ankhefenmut holds a
series of important titles that explain his presence on a
royal building; these include "Overseer of Secrets in the

Memphis Temple" (ḥry-sštȝ m ḥw.t-kȝ ptḥ), "Scribe of the Temple of the Estate of Ptah" (sš ḥw.t-pr ptḥ), "Counter of the Cattle of the Estate of Ptah" (ḥsb.w kȝw m pr ptḥ), and "Prophet of Ptah" (ḥm-nṯr ptḥ). The lintel's other half, also in the Carnegie collection, has a similar inscription.

The main temple in Memphis was dedicated to Ptah, a deity always depicted wearing a tightly wrapped garment and close-fitting cap and carrying a scepter that combines the hieroglyphs for "stability" and "dominion." Ptah was a creator god who was the central figure in one version of the ancient Egyptian myth explaining the world's creation. He was the only patron of craftsmen and, as such, was believed to be the source for ancient Egyptian civilization. Memphis, his city, was the earliest ancient Egyptian capital, built as legend dictates by Egypt's first pharaoh Menes (probably equatable with 'Aha). Located at the Delta's apex where Upper and Lower Egypt meet, Memphis was strategically located and remained the capital for all of ancient Egyptian history. Because Memphis was the focus of Egypt's administrative bureaucracy and generally supported the principal state workshops that produced objects for the pharaoh, it was literally the center of Egyptian culture.

60.

Coffin of a Chantress of Amun

(gessoed wood, paint)

Dynasty XXI (ca. 1070–945 B.C.)
Provenience unknown
Lid and base: length 191 cm; width 50 cm; height 62 cm
ACC. 1-1b (lid)
ACC. 1-1c (base)

The function of the ancient Egyptian coffins was to protect the mummy which housed the deceased's *ka* (spirit). This coffin's inscription and decoration indicate that it was made for a woman possessing the title "Chantress of Amun." The lid portrays a woman wearing earrings, a broad collar, and a wig decorated with a floral garland and vultures; her arms are crossed just under the wig's lappets. Her title was common during the New Kingdom and Third Intermediate Period and was often given to upper-class women who served as temple singers. On funerary equipment, the owner's name generally follows the title. On this coffin, however, spaces exist where the

60

61

individual's name should appear. This suggests that the coffin was not made specifically for this woman, but had been selected from stock probably shortly after her death. For reasons unknown, her name was never inscribed in the prepared places.

Both the lid and the base are embellished with vignettes depicting offerings and various gods, most of whom are associated with the Osirian cycle of rebirth. The bright yellow background color is common on coffins from this period. The close-up shows a priest presenting offer-

60. Detail

ings to the bovine form of Hathor. Here Hathor comes forth to receive the offerings from the western mountain where she protects cemeteries. The inscription reveals offering formulae dedicated to several gods including Re-Horakhty, Isis, and Nephthys.

The woman's mummy is so badly damaged that radiographic analyses were uninformative. Inside the coffin, among the mummy's remains, fragments of a floral wreath made from woven leaves, grass, and flowers were recovered. The floral arrangement was probably laid across the mummy's chest just before the priests sealed the coffin.

61.

Decorated Coffin Fragment

(gessoed wood, paint)

Probably Dynasty XXI (ca. 1070–945 B.C.)
Provenience unknown
Length 48 cm; width 22 cm
ACC. 9074-2429

Whenever possible, the ancient Egyptians decorated their coffins with scenes and inscriptions designed to provide the deceased with the necessary protection and guarantees for immortality in the afterlife. The hieroglyphic texts arranged in neat columns on this coffin fragment invoke several funerary deities including Osiris and Ptah-Sokar. The scene on the right is a classic illustration showing the deceased and his *ba* (a human-headed falcon) presenting an offering to one of these deities. The scene on the left, however, is less common. Here a member of the funeral party performs a step in the Opening-of-the-Mouth ceremony on the deceased, who is depicted as a mummy standing before his tomb chapel. The slanted wavy lines in the bottom left-hand corner depict a hill, and the red dots are a convention indicating sand. Thus this tomb and its chapel are situated on the edge of the low desert. Illustrations like this on coffins, papyri, and tomb paintings confirm what Egyptologists have learned from archaeological sites: Whenever possible the Egyptians preferred to locate their tombs in the dry low desert overlooking their settlements on the floodplain.

Third Intermediate and Late Periods

79

62.

Ba on a Coffin Fragment

(gessoed wood, paint)

Dynasty XXI (ca. 1070–945 B.C.)
Provenience unknown
Length 33 cm; width 27 cm
ACC. 2983-6551

For the ancient Egyptians, a person possessed many qualities, the most important of which were (1) the body, (2) the *ka* or vital life force, (3) the *ba*, (4) the *akh* or immortal spirit, and (5) the name. The *ba* was spirit-like, most often depicted, as on this object, as a human-headed bird. Unlike the *ka*, which came into being at the time of a person's birth, the *ba* appears to have been more important in the afterlife. The *ba* could travel with the sun barque across the sky on its daily journey or leave the tomb and visit the world of the living, returning each night to rejoin the deceased. The *ba* often was present alongside the deceased at his judgment before Osiris.

This fragment from a coffin's base depicts the *ba* with its wings outspread. Since this piece formed the canopy of an anthropoid coffin where the mummy's head lay, the *ba's* wings would have symbolically encircled the head, thereby protecting the deceased. The holes in the edges of the wood once held the dowels that locked this section to the coffin's side boards. The heads of two more gods are visible in the lower left and right corners. Their bodies would have continued on the coffin's sides. The decoration on the fragment's outer side has all but disappeared, exposing mud-brick plaster, thickened by straw, instead of the more common white gypsum plaster.

63.

Fragment from a Woman's Coffin

(gessoed wood, paint)

Dynasty XXI (ca. 1070–945 B.C.)
Provenience unknown
Length 46 cm; width 22.5 cm
ACC. 9074-2667

A falcon-headed god wearing a solar disk crown and seated upon a throne forms the primary decorative device on this painted coffin fragment. The inscription in front of the deity identifies him as Re-Horakhty-Atum, the god central in creation myths. To the ancient Egyptians, before the world appeared, only a dark, watery, void defined by eight gods and goddesses existed. Then Re, the sun god, rose out of this primordial water and established land. He gave birth to the god Shu and the goddesses Tefnet and Maat, and in some versions his tears became mankind. Thus divine cosmic order came into being.

Re had several aspects: Khepri, the morning; Horakhty, the midday; and Atum, the afternoon. Although Re-Horakhty-Atum was not a funerary god, during Dynasty XXI (ca. 1070–945 B.C.) with increasing frequency he replaced Osiris in the traditional offering formula. This shift accounts for his presence on this piece.

Although many ancient Egyptian coffins were decorated, the brightly colored and elaborately embellished

Third Intermediate Period coffins seem to have been particular favorites of late nineteenth- and early twentieth-century art collectors. Of the many hundreds of coffin fragments of this type, most show complete scenes or figures of gods; rarely do we see, for example, incomplete portions of two scenes. This observation suggests that during the early days of collecting, when someone located a coffin outside of an archaeological excavation, he carefully chopped it up into vignettes. The finder knew he could realize a greater profit from several pieces than from one whole object. This fragment of an anthropoid coffin, intended for a woman, is such a piece.

63

64.
Jar with a Bes-Image
(ceramic)

Third Intermediate Period (ca. 1070–653 B.C.)
Provenience unknown
Height 13 cm; diameter 6.4 cm
ACC. 9007-48

The potter who made this wide-mouthed jar in a simple ovoid shape rendered it more interesting by applying small pieces of clay to form a face. Although this visage is quite schematic, many other jars depict the same features in greater detail, allowing Egyptologists to identify this face as one of a group of very similar gods collectively known as the Bes-image. In the Third Intermediate Period, the Bes-image was a male figure merging the features of an achondroplastic dwarf and a lion (see drawing).

Although occasionally depicted on temple walls taking part in royal birthing scenes, the Bes-image was most frequently associated with the ancient Egyptian home. The deities represented by the Bes-image had as their primary responsibility the protection of women during pregnancy and childbirth. They were also the guardians of newborn infants. Bes-images also frequently served as the general protectors of a household against dangers, both imagined (such as malevolent spirits) and real (including scorpions and poisonous snakes). This explains the use

64

Third Intermediate and Late Periods

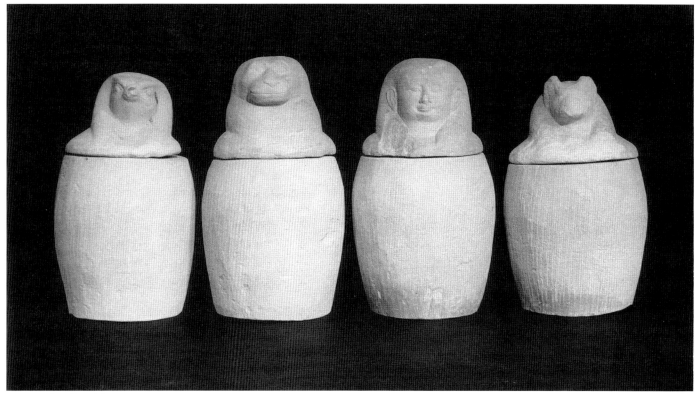

65 a-d: Left to right

of the Bes-image as a decorative element on many objects of daily life such as furniture, ceramic vessels, cosmetic equipment, headrests, and amulets. When the Bes-image appears on vessels, the interpretation is unclear. Most likely the presence of the Bes-image on jars was simply another way to associate these gods with a family's abode. The possibility remains, however, that these vessels had a function within a childbirthing ritual that is now unknown.

65.
Set of Canopic Jars

(limestone)
Dynasty XXVI (ca. 664–525 B.C.)
Provenience unknown

---

a. Height 27 cm; diameter 13 cm
ACC. 15673-5

c. Height 29 cm; diameter 13 cm
ACC. 15673-2

b. Height 28.5 cm; diameter
  13 cm
ACC. 15673-3

d. Height 26.5 cm; diameter
  14.3 cm
ACC. 15673-4

The ancient Egyptians knew that the internal organs were the first parts of a corpse to decompose, thus speeding the body's decay. Early in the mummification process of a human body, the embalmers removed the stomach, lungs, liver, and intestines through a slit made in the abdomen. These organs were mummified, using the same process performed on the body. When finished, each organ was placed in its own stoppered jar made from stone, pottery, wood, or occasionally faience. Canopic jars, as we call them, are known from the Old Kingdom (ca. 2750–2250 B.C.), and by the Middle Kingdom (ca. 2025 B.C.) certain gods and goddesses protected the four organs. The gods, known collectively as the sons of Horus, were each responsible for protecting a specific organ. During the late New Kingdom (1295–1070 B.C.), each lid in a set of canopic jars came to represent one of the Four Sons of Horus. From early Dynasty XVIII (ca. 1479) on, a jar's contents, its specific protective god, and its owner's name were often identified by an inscription on the container's surface.

This set of canopic jars clearly illustrates the falcon head of Qebehsenef, the baboon identifying Hapy, the human-headed Imset, and the jackal distinguishing Duamutef. Three jars are lined inside with a pitch-like substance, probably intended to keep resins and ointments in the organ packets from leaking through the porous limestone and staining the jars' surfaces. It is unlikely that these jars were ever inscribed and perhaps they were never finished.

66.
Amulets

66a–h: Clockwise from top left

a. Wedjet-Eye
(faience)
Late Period (ca. 664–332 B.C.)
Sharona
Length 6 cm; width 5 cm
ACC. 2400-29

b. Heart
(glass)
New Kingdom–Late Period
  (ca. 1539–332 B.C.)
Provenience unknown
Length 1.6 cm; width 1.1 cm
ACC. 33898-2

c. Djed-Pillar
(steatite)
Late Period? (ca. 664–332 B.C.)
Abydos, D66
Length 1.7 cm; width 0.8 cm
ACC. 1917-132

d. Bes-image
(faience)
Early Dynasty XVIII, reigns of
  Hatshepsut and Tuthmosis III
  (ca. 1539–1425 B.C.)
Abydos, D116
Length 2.6 cm; width 1.2 cm
ACC. 1917-40

e. Anubis
(faience)
Dynasty XX (ca. 1185–1070 B.C.)
Abydos, D28a
Length 2.5; width 0.6 cm
ACC. 1662-34

f. Re-Horakhty
(faience)
Early Dynasty XVIII, reigns of
  Hatshepsut and Tuthmosis III
  (ca. 1539–1425 B.C.)
Abydos, D116
Length 3 cm; width 1 cm; depth
  1.6 cm
ACC. 1917-61

g. Human-headed Heart
(faience)
Dynasty XX (ca. 1185–1070 B.C.)
Abydos, D28a
Length 4.3 cm; width 2.4 cm
ACC. 1662-43

h. Winged Scarab in Three Pieces
(faience)
Late Period (ca. 664–332 B.C.)
Provenience unknown
Complete length 12.1 cm;
  scarab: length 5.7 cm; width
  3.7 cm
ACC. 2983-6719

The need to prevent disaster or avert negative powers and the desire to promote well-being are compelling forces in any culture. The ancient Egyptians possessed many beliefs, focused around their gods and goddesses, designed to protect themselves and foster security. Amulets, or charms, are tangible images of these convictions. The ancient Egyptians believed amulets could aid them because the charms embodied the gods or goddesses who were responsible for the culture's survival.

This group of amulets illustrates only a small fraction of the various types known from ancient Egypt. A person's wealth and needs determined a talisman's material and quality and occasionally size. Most amulets were made from faience, glass, or semiprecious stone, but more expensive substances such as gold, silver, lapis lazuli, and ivory are known. The Bes-image (figure 66d), Anubis (figure 66e), and Re-Horakhty (figure 66f) belong to the largest group of amulets, those depicting a god or goddess. A talisman from this group brought the owner under the aegis of a particular deity. The *djed*-pillar (figure 66c), winged scarab (figure 66h), and the *wedjet*-eye (figure 66a) feature specific powers associated with a deity. The *djed*-pillar, a symbol of endurance and stability, was identified with Osiris, the god of the underworld. The winged scarab represented the concept of eternal rebirth embodied in Khepri, the morning sun. The *wedjet*-eye was the god Horus's left eye, which was healed by the ibis-headed god Thoth after Seth, Horus's uncle, had stolen it. It was one of the most powerful protective symbols.

Another group of amulets illustrates articles desired in the afterlife, for example, a head, a name, or food offerings. Possession of this type of amulet permanently secured the object for the deceased. The human-headed heart (figure 66g) and the small heart (figure 66b) belong to this category. They portray the human heart, which the Egyptians considered to be the source of a person's intelligence and emotion, and essential for eternal life. Other known categories of amulets include those in the shape of hieroglyphs that represent a power desired by the deceased, for example, *ankh* (life) or *shen* (encircle). A few amulets, including those shaped as crowns or shells, stood for forces not directly associated with a particular god.

Third Intermediate and Late Periods

Most amulets are recovered from the wrappings of mummies or in containers in tombs, although small numbers of amulets have been found in settlements. The deceased used amulets to prevent dangers encountered during the journey into the afterlife, an existence eagerly anticipated but perilous to enter. Occasionally a sculpture or tomb illustration shows a man or woman wearing a charm, but overall we have few examples of what Egyptians may have worn to protect themselves during their lifetimes.

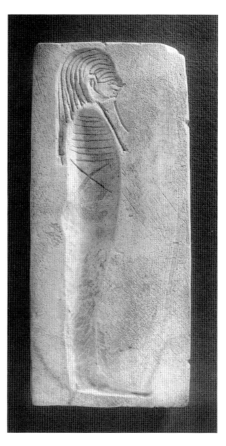

67.

Gold Foil Mold

(limestone)

Third Intermediate–Late Periods (ca. 1070–332 B.C.)
Provenience unknown
Length 11.5 cm; width 5.1 cm
ACC. 2983-6705

An artisan made this mold from a small chunk of stone by leveling and polishing smooth its surface, while only roughly finishing the back. He then carved a mummiform figure, probably representing one of the Four Sons of Horus, in sunk relief. By hammering a sheet of gold into this form, a craftsman transferred the design to the metal. Next he probably trimmed the sheet bearing the figure and punched holes in its corners. The finished product was sewn onto mummy wrappings or a beaded net destined to enshroud a body.

The use of metals in ancient Egypt began in the Predynastic Period (ca. 4500–3100 B.C.). By the Early Dynastic Period (ca. 3100 B.C.), the Egyptians were regularly manipulating gold and smelting copper ores. They collected gold as granules in gravels or quarried it as veins through quartz found in the Eastern Desert and Nubia, while they mined copper ores along with turquoise in the Eastern Desert and Sinai. Quarrymen removed impurities at the mine sites. Gold, for example, arrived at the treasuries as bars or rings ready for distribution to the workshops. Bronze technology appeared after about 2025 B.C. and soon became very important. The capability to manufacture iron was widespread only from Dynasty XXVI (ca. 664 B.C.) on.

Craftsmen skilled in metallurgy are well documented in tomb illustrations from both the Old Kingdom (ca. 2750–2250 B.C.) and the New Kingdom (ca. 1539–1070 B.C.). Gold workers practiced their craft alongside other jewelry makers, while artisans working in copper or bronze had separate quarters. Artifacts, many from royal burials, illustrate the technical mastery achieved by goldsmiths. The various techniques included hammering, engraving, raising, casting in the lost-wax process, gold foil production, gilding, granulation, and cloisonné.

68.

Statuettes of Gods

(bronze)

---

a. Osiris
Dynasty XXVI (ca. 664–525 B.C.)
Abydos, Osiris temple
Height 22 cm; width 6.3 cm
ACC. 2231-19

b. Isis and Horus
Late Period–Ptolemaic Period (ca. 664–30 B.C.)

Faiyum?
Height 19.1 cm; width 4.3 cm
ACC. 2400-3

c. Maat
Late Period (ca. 664–332 B.C.)
Provenience unknown
Height 7 cm; width 1.6 cm; depth 2 cm
ACC. 33898-4

Few Egyptians were permitted into temples, which were reserved for the priests and a privileged few. Most people regularly worshiped at domestic and local shrines. On occasions, however, when someone desired to pay homage to one of the principal deities who safeguarded Egypt, the donation of a gift allowed limited access to the cult temple and divine protection.

A person offered votive objects for several reasons. Frequently, the supplicant wanted the god to forgive a recent moral or ritual offense, or to award a desired goal, such as having a child or curing an illness. These votive gifts took a variety of forms including statuettes, stelae, symbolic objects, and replicas of human ears (so the deity could hear the plea). The quality of votive offerings ranges from highly accomplished to crude, reflecting the economic status of the various donors including the pharaoh, nobles, and probably members of the "middle" class. Small statuettes in bronze or faience representing a particular deity or his or her sacred animal form were among the most common votive gifts.

Osiris (figure 68a) and Isis (here with the infant Horus, figure 68b) are two deities whose statuettes were found in shrines throughout Egypt. Osiris, ruler of the underworld, and his loyal wife Isis figured prominently in one of the few, but most popular, religious myths. They were, therefore, potent deities to whom supplication during crises made a great deal of sense to the ancient Egyptians. The statuette of Isis wears a vulture crown, the details of which are still well preserved in the bronze, surmounted by the sun disk and a pair of cow's horns. This statuette represents Isis in her role as a mother holding the infant Horus in her lap ready to nurse. The cult dedicated to Isis as Horus's mother became very popular in the Ptolemaic Period (ca. 332–30 B.C.) and subsequently, under the Romans (after 30 B.C.), achieved substantial acceptance in southern Europe.

Personified by the goddess of the same name (figure 68c), *maat* was the ideal state of the orderly Egyptian universe and society that was established by the creator god and carefully maintained by tradition and ritual. Maat embodied this concept through truth, justice, and order. Although the pharaoh had the greatest responsibility for the continuation of *maat* by carrying out temple rituals and leading an exemplary life, all ancient Egyptians had an obligation to conduct their lives according to society's conventions of behavior. When the pharaoh failed in his duties, Egypt's security was at stake; when people failed at their responsibilities, their eternal life and perhaps even that of their families were in jeopardy.

Maat had her own priesthood and temples. Pharaohs, however, were often depicted offering a Maat statuette to

68a-b: Left to right

68c

Third Intermediate and Late Periods

85

another deity in his or her temple. In these reliefs, the Maat statuette symbolizes all material things offered to a god during the cult's daily ritual. Maat is always depicted as a goddess, often seated with her knees drawn up to her chest, wearing a crown with a single ostrich feather. On figure 68c, the feather is now missing. The throne is decorated with Hathor capitals and uraei.

69.
Palette for Ink

(faience)

Late Period (ca. 664–332 B.C.)
Provenience unknown
Length 7.1 cm; width 3.3 cm
ACC. 33898-3

A scribe once owned this simple, but elegant palette and used it to hold his cakes of red and black ink. Each depression is surrounded by a *shen* hieroglyph and the pair are enclosed by a cartouche, a larger version of the *shen* sign. Both the *shen* glyph and the cartouche represent coiled ropes meaning "that which the sun [Re] encircles." Since the written word was a gift from the gods, the hieroglyphs on the palette reinforced the divine nature of what was produced by using the ink.

The scribe's basic equipment included reed brushes and their case, a pot for water, and a palette with two containers holding red and black ink. This kit was so universal that when depicted as a set it formed the hieroglyph that Egyptologists translate as "scribe," "writing," or "to write" (𓏞). Scribes used their writing kits to inscribe papyrus, ceramic, stone, and occasionally linen. Papyrus, paper made by the ancient Egyptians from a reedy plant, was produced as early as Dynasty I (ca. 3100–2900 B.C.). Administrative and scientific documents, letters, literature and poetry, and religious texts including the "Book of the Dead" were recorded on papyrus. When scribes needed "scratch paper" to record information needed for only a short time, they used ceramic sherds and stone fragments, now called ostraca, and small slabs of plastered wood. Papyrus was too costly to use for anything but the most permanent documents.

To write, the scribe dipped the reed brush into the water pot and then rubbed the brush in the cake of ink. Black ink was made from carbon; red ink, from crushed ocher, a soft iron ore. Each substance was mixed with

69

gum and dried into a cake that subsequently rested in its own dish in the palette. Most texts were done in black ink, whereas red ink was largely used to write dates, headings, and opening words. One dip into the ink generally allowed the scribe to write several hieroglyphs before the ink ran dry. Mistakes caught early could be removed with a damp cloth or a quick lick of the tongue. Mistakes left too long could only be erased by cutting out the offending section of papyrus and gluing in a new piece.

70.
Ptah-Sokar-Osiris Statuette

(gessoed wood, paint)

Late Period (ca. 664–332 B.C.)
Provenience unknown
Height 54.8 cm; width 17 cm; depth 30.4 cm
ACC. 9074-2462a

This statuette represents a funerary deity whose identity is a composite of the three ancient Egyptian gods, Ptah, Sokar, and Osiris. Statuettes of this god appear in the New Kingdom (ca. 1539–1070 B.C.), but his popularity increased significantly during the Late Period. The conflation of these three gods occurred because their domains overlapped. Ptah was associated with vegetation and the creation of the world, similar to the role of rebirth assigned to Osiris. Sokar, a desert deity who came to be associated with cemeteries, converged with Osiris' realm as lord of the underworld and the dead.

Ptah-Sokar-Osiris statuettes, often bearing traditional offering formulae, were placed in tombs to assist in the resurrection of the deceased's body. A statuette's base was frequently shaped like a sarcophagus and either the figure's body or base could be hollow. These compartments often contained papyri inscribed with spells from the collection known as "Coming Forth by Day" or mummified remains; this Ptah-Sokar-Osiris statuette's base is solid with the front end shaped to resemble a sarcophagus. Often falcons, symbolizing Sokar, rested on these sarcophagus-like bases.

The Carnegie statuette was well crafted, although much of the gesso and paint has been lost from its wooden form. Very little of the inscription remains and the area containing the name of the person for whom this statuette was made has been lost forever. Only the brightness of the paint and the remnants of detail on the statuette indicate that at one time it was an attractive as well as functional piece of funerary equipment.

71.

Alabastron

(glass)

Late Period (ca. 664–332 B.C.)
Provenience unknown
Height 11.2 cm; diameter 3.3 cm
ACC. 29825

The few examples of ancient Egyptian glass that are dated prior to the New Kingdom (ca. 1539 B.C.) were probably the result of accidentally overfiring faience. Egyptologists believe that the Egyptians acquired the technology for large-scale glass manufacture from western Asia around 1500 B.C., when Egyptian military conquest established extensive contacts with that region. Egyptian craftsmen rapidly became proficient in glassmaking, perfecting the techniques. Glass was very common in Dynasty XVIII–XIX (ca. 1539–1185 B.C.) and in the latter half of the first millennium B.C. Because the ancient Egyptians considered glass to be a precious material, it was reserved for use in jewelry, inlays, cosmetic containers, and occasionally small drinking cups. Little objects could be molded or cast, but most pieces, especially vessels, were core-made.

70

71

Third Intermediate and Late Periods

72

Blown glass was unknown in Egypt before the latter part of the Roman Period (ca. A.D. 300).

Ancient glass was made from silica, calcium carbonate, and an alkali. Silica was obtained from sand, which in Egypt often contains a naturally occurring calcium compound. Natron, the same substance used in faience manufacture and mummification, was a common alkali. Therefore, the materials necessary for making glass were easily available within the country. Many of the coloring agents for glass were also local; these included copper salts (blue-green, green, and red), manganese (purple), and antimony and lead (yellow). Others, such as cobalt (dark blue) and oxide of tin (white), must have been imported.

This alabastron, a bag-shaped jar with two handles, is core-made. Such vessels were manufactured by wrapping molten glass around a core of clay or dung attached to a rod. When glass threads of different colors were dragged along the surface of the vessel, patterns could be added to the body. For this jar, an artisan trailed yellow and turquoise glass threads in zigzag lines and parallel bands around the vessel. Then, while the vessel was still warm, it was rolled and pressed on a surface to bind and flatten the exterior; this is called marvering. Additional trails of glass were used to make the rim and handles. After the vessel cooled, the excess glass, the rod, and the core were removed and the finished piece polished. This alabastron probably held perfume or another costly liquid.

72.

Sistrum

(bronze)

Late Period (ca. 664–332 B.C.)
Provenience unknown
Length 16.2 cm; width 4.5 cm
ACC. 9074-2251

Music, both singing and the playing of instruments, was a necessary part of temple ritual. The most common musical instrument depicted in religious reliefs is the sistrum, a rattle-like instrument. Sistra, played only by women, were shaken to frighten away evil and soothe any anger a god might have. As a result, they are often elaborately embellished with imagery believed efficacious in the eternal struggle against chaos.

This sistrum shows many such images. The two-sided face depicts Hathor, who is a daughter of the sun god, Re, and a mother goddess often possessing a bovine form. Since she is also associated with love, dancing, and music, the sistrum is one of her sacred symbols. Hathor's head rests atop a palmiform column because palms were sacred to her father, Re. On either side of the handle, uraei (aroused cobras) rest on Hathor's broad collar and rise to touch the rattle's outer edge. Uraei are protective symbols of Re; here their different crowns represent Upper and Lower Egypt. Above each cobra, a Bes-image, wearing a feathered crown, represents any of several protective gods. Like the cobras, the Bes-images guard the sistrum; Bes-images are also associated with music during the late Pharaonic Period.

A cat sits above Hathor's head and represents Bastet, the goddess of peace and also an aspect of Hathor, while two couchant lions, one of which is now missing, were found at the handle's base. The artisan may have intended to contrast two aspects of Hathor, the potentially destructive lioness and the gentle cat. However, the original presence of two lions suggests instead that they portrayed the guardians of the horizon, where Re appeared daily. The rattle's edges once continued forming a loop; bars filled with disks stretched between the two sides of the loop. When shaken, the rattling disks would have made the sistrum's distinctive noise.

73.
Imhotep Statuette
(bronze)

73

Late Period (ca. 664–332 B.C.)
Provenience unknown
Height 14.3 cm; width 3.5 cm
ACC. 11983-12

On rare occasions in ancient Egypt, a man could achieve so high a status during his lifetime that sometime after his death his feats became legendary and he was deified. Imhotep, the chief architect of Pharaoh Djoser (ca. 2700 B.C.), was such a man. He was the highest official in Djoser's administration and designed and built the first stone structure, the Step Pyramid complex. About two thousand years after his death, his legend developed into a traditional cult, and several places including Saqqara, Deir el-Medina, and Philae had shrines for him with the attendant rituals and personnel. Small bronze statues such as this one represented Imhotep and were dedicated by the faithful at his shrines. He is always portrayed as a seated scribe, close shaven, holding an open papyrus scroll across his lap. This depiction reflects his association with wisdom and learning. In addition, he was venerated as a god identified with medicine, a solver of personal problems, and fertility.

74.
Votive Clepsydra
(faience)

Late Period–Ptolemaic Period (ca. 664–30 B.C.)
Provenience unknown
Height 11 cm; width 3.3 cm; depth 6.6 cm
ACC. 33898-1

By day most ancient Egyptians estimated time by the sun's position. Because of requirements of temple ritual, priests relied on shadow clocks for a more precise reading of daytime intervals. Temple rituals continued at night, however, requiring alternatives to measuring the sun's movement. Two methods were devised to track the nighttime hours: the movement of the stars and the clepsydra, or water clock. The first-known Egyptian clepsydrae were bowls marked by twelve divisions (hours of the night) and filled with water. At the base of the vessel, a tiny hole allowed the water to drain at a constant speed. As the water passed each division, it marked an hour's passage. When the bowl was empty, the night was over and the new day begun.

This clepsydra is a votive piece. Its small size and lack of markings preclude its use as a true water clock, although it could have functioned symbolically. Water poured into the hollowed pillar exits through the hole in the stairs below the baboon's feet into the trough.

74

75

The hole, however, is large for the object's size, causing the filled pillar to empty in less than twenty seconds. This also supports its identification as a votive clepsydra. The function of the knob above the figure of the baboon is unknown, but each of the column's three other sides once possessed one. The baboon, emerging from one side of the pillar, is sacred to Thoth, a god most often represented as an ibis-headed man, whose responsibilities included the moon, writing and record keeping, and time. This object was probably donated by an individual to a temple or shrine, perhaps one dedicated to Thoth.

75.

Plaque with a Pharaoh's Head

(limestone)

Dynasty XXX–early Ptolemaic Period (ca. 380–246 B.C.)
Provenience unknown
Length 16.7 cm; width 14.1 cm; thickness 2.8 cm
ACC. 33897-1

Despite the extensive damage suffered by this limestone plaque, enough of the fine low relief carving survives to demonstrate that the subject was the head of a king wearing a close-fitting helmet surmounted in the front by an uraeus (aroused cobra). The face's style and the uraeus's double loop both suggest a Dynasty XXX to early Ptolemaic Period date. The erosion of the eye and chin and a crack across the face (now repaired) make it impossible to identify the specific king represented.

The reverse side was also worked, but the carver had only begun to outline the three mummiform figures still visible. Their form, position (two figures face left; the third faces right), and costume suggest that the artisan intended to represent the Four Sons of Horus, although there is only enough room for three. The plaque's edges are eroded, except for the lower left where the original smoothness is still visible.

Small rectangular plaques similar to this one are well documented. Although they often show images of a pharaoh's head, they sometimes depict deities, queens, or animals. When a context for these plaques is known, they appear to have served as votive offerings to deities. However, because some of the images are unfinished, such as the reverse of this example, the possibility cannot be overlooked that these plaques were originally sculptors' or artisans' models that were subsequently donated to a divinity.

76.
Mummy of a Child

(human remains, linen, painted cartonnage)

Dynasty XXX–early Ptolemaic Period (ca. 380–250 B.C.)
Abydos, E422
Length 74.5 cm; width 21.7 cm; depth 19.3 cm
ACC. 4698-1

During the field season of 1911–12, T. Eric Peet excavated a cemetery at Abydos that spanned four thousand
years. In the only intact vaulted tomb, Peet found twelve
individuals. The seven adults were in limestone sarcophagi while the five children lay in wooden coffins. Each
mummy was elaborately decorated with six cartonnage
pieces all very similar in style: a mask, a breastplate, three
panels over the legs, and a foot covering.

This child's body, one of five from this tomb, is securely
wrapped in plainweave linen. Its mask depicts a face
whose wig is surmounted by a winged scarab beetle pushing the sun disk. The breastplate illustrates a broad collar, while the foot covering represents a child's sandaled
feet. The three panels over the lower part of the body
depict the Four Sons of Horus, Nut, and an *ankh* flanked
by minor deities respectively.

Radiographic imaging (x-rays) provided additional information about the mummy. The bones have remained
largely in place; the x-rays show the child to be lying on
its back, its arms at its sides with its head fallen slightly
forward so the chin rests on the chest. The child was
assigned a chronological age of eight or nine following a
detailed study of wrist development. The head is the only
section of the body where an anomaly is visible. The
child's cranium appears enlarged (megacephaly); this may
reflect a medical problem although cause of death is undetermined. Some cranial distortion may have occurred,
however, during the radiographic process since the
wrapped body could not be adjusted to a position best
suited for x-raying. The rest of the body appears normal,
but no determination of sex is possible.

Ptolemaic Period, CIRCA 332–30 B.C.

and

Roman Period, CIRCA 30 B.C.–A.D. 395

INTRODUCTION

By defeating the Persians in 332 B.C., Alexander the Great acquired Egypt, beginning the Ptolemaic Period (ca. 332–30 B.C.). Recognizing that he needed local Egyptian support, he made himself acceptable by exploiting Egyptian traditions, especially religious ones. This attitude continued after Alexander's death, when a Macedonian general named Ptolemy appropriated Egypt and eventually assumed the throne as Ptolemy I. Early Ptolemaic rule was largely peaceful and prosperous, although Egyptian Greeks possessed a higher status than native Egyptians. During the Ptolemaic Period, Alexandria was founded and became the most important city in Egypt. Also the kings erected many new temples, like those at Edfu, Philae, and Dendera. Under the Ptolemies and later the Romans, some gods were popularized; these included Isis and Serapis, who was a Ptolemaic amalgam of the Egyptian gods Osiris and Apis. These cults rapidly spread outside Egypt throughout the Aegean and Asia Minor.

Over time, the Ptolemies had increasing problems controlling Egypt, especially in the Theban area, as well as their other foreign territories. They turned for assistance to Rome, an empire already attracted to the region by its productive farmland.

Kleopatra VII (Kleopatra the Great) was Egypt's last Ptolemaic ruler. A bright, well-educated, and ambitous woman, she had matured during a politically unstable period. In her quest for power and a secure throne, she manipulated first Julius Caesar and then Marc Anthony into aiding her political ambitions. During this period, Roman influence over Egypt grew. Octavian defeated Anthony and Kleopatra VII at Actium in 31 B.C., causing them subsequently to commit suicide, thereby ending the Ptolemaic dynasty. Egypt, then, rapidly became part of Rome's empire (Roman Period, 30 B.C.–A.D. 395).

Initially Octavian, now called Emperor Augustus, made Egypt his private domain. Egyptian grain was being sent at this time to the rest of Rome's empire. Although Roman officials, supported by their own legions, taxed the inhabitants as heavily as possible, Egypt remained relatively well off through the second century before it began to decline. Throughout the Roman Period, only a few emperors, such as Trajan, Hadrian, and Diocletian, visited Egypt. The emperors did, however, continue to build monuments along traditional lines. With the appearance of Christianity, ancient Egyptian culture slowly perished. Ancient Egypt's history officially ended with the beginning of the Byzantine Empire (A.D. 395).

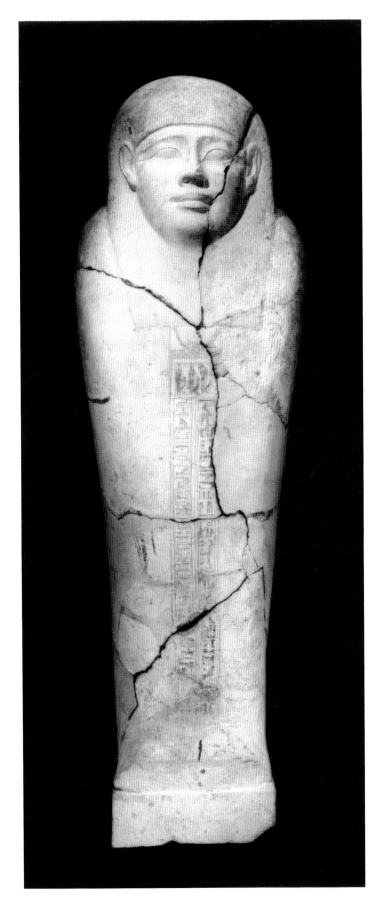

77.
Anthropoid Sarcophagus

(limestone, paint)

Early Ptolemaic Period (ca. 332–200 B.C.)
Abydos, Cemetery D?
Length 200 cm; width 66 cm; height 36.5 cm
ACC. 1917-472

During the late Second Intermediate Period (ca. 1600 B.C.), a new type of wooden coffin in anthropoid or human shape made its initial appearance in Egypt. This configuration rapidly gained popularity and by the end of Dynasty XVIII (ca. 1295 B.C.) was even being made in stone. Stone sarcophagi were uncommon among nonroyal Egyptians, however, until the Late Period (ca. 664–332 B.C.). Then and in the subsequent Ptolemaic Period, even moderately prosperous people were commissioning them for their burials.

This heavily reconstructed sarcophagus belonged to Mehetdiesnakht *(mḥt-dỉ.s-nḫt)*, a woman buried at the sacred site of Abydos. The piece was never finished; the necklace and its attendant inscription are only partially carved and painted. Her necklace is a pectoral with figures of the deities Osiris, Isis, and Nephthys seated from right to left. The inscription descends in two columns from the pectoral down the front of her body. Both Mehetdiesnakht and her mother, Astweret *(ȝs.t-wr.t)*, had the title "Sistrum Player of Khentiamentiu" *(ỉḥy ḫnty-ỉmn.tyw)*, indicating that they played rattles during rituals performed at Osiris' temple at Abydos. Her father, Hor? *(ḥr-?)*, bore the titles "Priest of the Osiris Temple" *(ḥsk.w)* and "Prophet for the Cult of Bastet in Abydos" *(ḥm-nṯr bȝs.t.t ḥry-ỉb ȝbḏw)*. The inscriptions suggest that the family's income was principally, if not entirely, earned through its involvement with the temple. Since all of the titles are minor, however, these people were probably part of the "middle" class, not wealthy nobility.

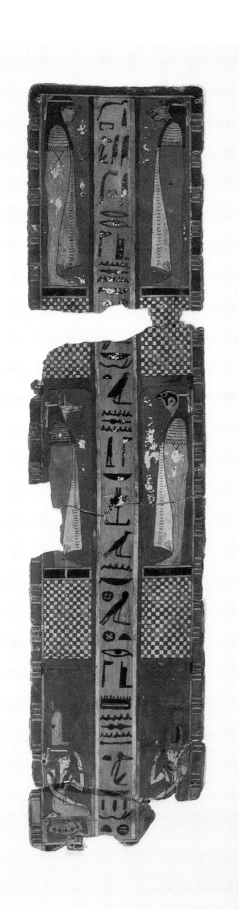

78.

Decorated Panel for a Mummy

(linen, plaster, paint)

Ptolemaic Period (ca. 332–30 B.C.)
Sedment
Length 67 cm; width 15.2 cm
ACC. 4209-15

This panel or apron was once part of a cartonnage set, made from plastered linen, that adorned the front of a mummy. In addition to panels, generally positioned over the abdomen or legs, these sets often included a mask, a breastplate, and a foot covering (see entry 76). Each piece in a set generally repeated decorative elements that embellished coffins: Head pieces were faces, breastplates imitated floral collars, and foot coverings were decorated with feet sometimes shod in sandals. The lower body panels generally depicted deities important in funeral ritual and the afterlife. Here the Four Sons of Horus, the same gods consistently decorating canopic jar lids after the New Kingdom, protect the deceased. Below, although a portion of the panel is missing, Isis (left) and Nephthys, guardian goddesses, mourn the deceased by raising their arms before their faces. The fine brush strokes used to outline and detail the figures show the great control of a highly accomplished painter.

79.
Incense Burner

(bronze)

Ptolemaic Period (ca. 332–30 B.C.)
Qasr el-Banât
Height 8.3 cm; length 36.8 cm
ACC. 1948-3

Recovered from excavations at the town of Qasr el-Banât in the Faiyum, this incense burner probably served as cultic equipment in a local temple. The censor is shaped like a human forearm with a falcon-headed finial. Other incense burners and representations from temple reliefs allow us to reconstruct this object's missing components (see drawing). The finial for the burner's other end would have been an open hand with a palm faced up balancing a small bowl for kindling the incense. The wrist area would have been shaped like a papyrus flower. On the censor's stem, a figure representing a kneeling king in his role as chief priest wears a *nemes* headdress and a *shendyt* kilt. He presents a dish designed to hold incense pellets for future use. This censor type is known as early as Dynasty XI (ca. 2025–1979 B.C.), although its origin may be earlier as seen in representations on reliefs from private tombs in the late Old Kingdom (ca. 2565–2250 B.C.). Any inscription identifying a god's name or the royal or private benefactor who donated this incense burner to the temple has long since disappeared through damage caused by heavy corrosion found all over the object's surface.

The burning of incense was a crucial element in any ritual undertaken by temple priests and a necessary component of funeral rites. In a temple, the chief priest (either the king or his chosen representative) burned incense before the god's image to purify the air of all evil. The incense pellets, ignited in the bowl, released a fragrance believed to be the scent of the god himself. Temple ceremonies required the use of the highly prized, but

rare gum resins, such as frankincense and myrrh, found only in countries bordering the southern Red Sea. Therefore, frankincense and myrrh were principal trade items acquired by the Egyptians through their contacts in Nubia and Punt. When the ancient Egyptians were unable to secure these types of incense, resins obtained from the inhabitants of Syro-Palestine or the Aegean became a poor second choice. Their pungent smoke was far less pleasing than the fragrances of the gum resins.

80.
Animal Mummies

(animal remains, linen)
Roman Period (ca. 30 B.C.–A.D. 300)

a. Cat	*c.* Crocodile
Provenience unknown	Provenience unknown
Length 49.5 cm; diameter 9 cm	Length 32.2 cm; width 6 cm
ACC. 3677-4	ACC. 1867-4
b. Ibis	
Abydos	
Length 35 cm; width 13.5 cm	
ACC. 4918-3	

From the Predynastic Period (ca. 4500–3100 B.C.) throughout most of ancient Egyptian history (ca. 3100 B.C.–A.D. 300), animals played an important role in religion. Many Egyptian gods were identified with certain species of animals. The most important animals were the falcon, ibis, cow, bull, ram, lion, jackal, cobra, and scarab beetle, while the baboon, cat, goose, crocodile, vulture, mongoose, and several species of fish had less prominent roles. Often all members of a species were sacred; only a representative number, however, were cared for within the appropriate temple precinct. These animals were attended by priests and lived out their lives in relative comfort. After an animal's death, the priests mummified it so that it too could have eternal existence alongside its protector.

Prior to the Late Period (ca. 664–332 B.C.), only a small number of animals resided at each temple and the associated animal cemeteries were of modest size. At some point, the priests realized that they could increase a temple's income by selling mummified sacred animals to pilgrims as votive offerings (pledges to a god). As a result, during the Late and Ptolemaic Periods and into the Roman Period (ca. 664 B.C.–A.D. 300), ibises, falcons, cats,

79

80a

80b

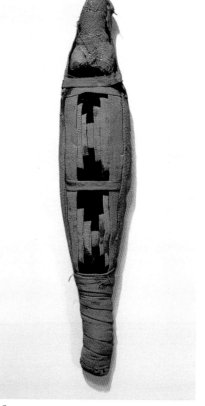

80c

crocodiles, and fish were mummified in vast numbers, resulting in the creation of enormous animal cemeteries. Since large numbers of animals were required, priests did not allow them to die of old age; instead most were slaughtered when they reached adulthood. Mummifying these sacred animals became an industry that supported the animals' caretakers, the embalmers, the priests undertaking the necessary temple rituals, and others.

Figure 80a is a mummy of an adult cat that died of a broken neck. Cats were sacred to Bastet, the goddess of peace, music, joy, and dancing who was an important deity in the Late Period. A similarly styled cat mummy, also in the collection (Accession 1764-4b), contains only two small nonfeline bones. Occasionally priests cheated, creating beautifully wrapped packages without actually mummifying an animal. An unsuspecting pilgrim may have paid a substantial sum for the privilege of donating this forged mummy to a temple.

An adult ibis whose neck, wings, and legs are tucked up together is under the bandages of figure 80b. Thoth, the god of the moon, writing and record keeping, and time, held the ibis in veneration. Roman embalmers often chose to wrap the dyed linen into this elaborate diamond-shaped pattern.

The ancient Egyptians possessed an ambivalent attitude toward the crocodile. The creature's strength and its habit of lying unseen below the water's surface waiting to attack the unsuspecting contributed to the fear and awe the Egyptians felt about this animal. In association with Sobek, a solar deity who fought the enemies of Re, the crocodile assumed one of its positive roles. The juvenile crocodile mummy shown in figure 80c probably comes from an animal cemetery in the Faiyum. Greek records indicate that large numbers of crocodiles were kept in the Faiyum and fed bread, burnt meat, and a mixture of honey and water, food that seems more extravagant than healthy.

81 a-b: Left to right

81.

Lamps

(ceramic)
Provenience unknown

a. Roman Period (ca. A.D. 50–200)
Length 10.2 cm; width 5 cm
ACC. 19458-29

b. Roman Period (ca. A.D. 150–300)
Length 8 cm; width 7.2 cm
ACC. 19458-30

Like most agriculturally based societies, the ancient Egyptians carried out most of their daily activities between sunrise and sunset. But after sunset or when they worked in tombs or performed rituals in a temple's interior, the Egyptians needed artificial light. Often they used oil lamps. During the Pharaonic Period (ca. 3100–332 B.C.), a common type of lamp consisted of a saucer filled with vegetable oil and salt (to reduce smoking) containing a floating wick. From archaeologically recovered examples, we know that both pottery and limestone were modeled into these simple shapes. Lamps could sit on any flat surface such as a table or a wall niche. Wooden floor stands that cradled a lamp between three pegs surmounting a column are also known.

During the Ptolemaic and Roman Periods, ceramic lamps were produced in large numbers with a variety of shapes and designs. In the Roman Period, potters frequently used molds instead of shaping their lamps on a wheel or by hand. Molds allowed duplication in large numbers of one object whose shape and design could then be easily copied by other craftsmen in different regions. Thus, many Roman lamps are of similar or virtually identical design.

These two lamps belong to types known from Roman settlements in Egypt including Karanis in the Faiyum. The lamp on the left (figure 81a) may represent a comic mask used in the theater. The mask has been molded, but the narrow base appears to be hand modeled. The lamp in marl clay (figure 81b) has the common frog and wheat design into which the holes for pouring the oil and holding the wick have been punched. This lamp was molded in two parts, the top and the base, that were then fitted together by hand. The base carries a potter's mark (![potter's mark]), possibly an *alpha* sign, a common mark stamped into bases during this period. Neither lamp appears to have been used, perhaps indicating their purpose solely as funerary items.

82.

Coffin for a Mummy

(gypsum? and mud plaster, paint)

Early to mid Roman Period (ca. A.D. 1–200)
Hawara?
Length 169 cm; width 47 cm; height 36.5 cm
ACC. 22266-1b

This brightly colored coffin contained the mummified body of an adult man. A demotic inscription found on the wig's lappets gives some genealogical information. The bright pink color with gilded details was a popular decorative scheme for coffins of Greek settlers in Egypt in the early Roman Period. The red and black crisscross pattern over the pink background imitates a beaded shroud,

82

82. Detail

a funerary decoration often found covering mummies. Coffins of this type were probably mass produced in workshops. First, the craftsmen spread a thin layer of plaster over a form which they then covered with a thick layer of mud plaster mixed with large amounts of straw. Next, they applied another thin layer of plaster, called gesso, to which they added more plaster modeled to form three-dimensional decorative elements such as the rosettes, the broad collar, and the winged Isis. Finally, the coffin was painted.

A face with a rosette diadem across the forehead dominates the upper portion of the coffin (see the close-up), while a large pectoral in the shape of a *ba* bird lies on the chest and painted feet wearing sandals adorn the base. Other motifs, including recognizable gods and goddesses, fill the area of the abdomen, legs, and the lower edges all the way around the coffin.

When donated to The Carnegie, the coffin contained a mummy covered with a gilded mask and a painted breastplate (Accession 22266-1a). Thin strips of linen were wound around the body in geometric patterns typical of the Roman Period. A resin? was painted over the wrappings, making a grid-like pattern. X-rays indicated that the mummy was a man who had died between the ages of thirty-five and fifty-five, but there were no signs of serious disease or how he died. The priests who mummified this man laid him out straight and crossed his arms on his chest.

The inscription suggests that the man was the son of Horpaheter (*ḥr-pȝ-ḥtr*) and the grandson of Pasherkhensu (*pȝ-šr-ḫnsw*), and died on "day 12" of the "fourth month of summer" of "Year 33" of an unnamed king.[1] The only Roman emperors with reigns that accommodate this regnal year are Augustus and Commodus.

1. I want to thank Richard Jasnow, of Würzburg, West Germany, for providing his translation of the demotic text, although any misinterpretation is my responsibility.

APPENDIX 1

Other Objects in The Walton Hall of Ancient Egypt

This list presents the objects exhibited in *The Walton Hall of Ancient Egypt* that were not included in this catalogue's entries. Objects are unprovenienced unless otherwise indicated.

Mold for Scarab Back
(ceramic)
New Kingdom (ca. 1539–1070 B.C.)
Length 3.9 cm; width 3.8 cm
ACC. Z9-414a

Mold with Tutankhamen's Cartouche
(ceramic)
New Kingdom (ca. 1539–1070 B.C.)
Length 3.8 cm; width 3 cm
ACC. Z9-414b

Mold for Wedjet*-eye Amulet*
(ceramic)
New Kingdom (ca. 1539–1070 B.C.)
Length 3.6 cm; width 3.5 cm
ACC. Z9-414c

Ear Stud
(glass)
Dynasty XVIII (ca. 1539–1295 B.C.)
Length 2.9 cm; diameter 1.4 cm
ACC. Z9-498c

Fragments from Floral Collar
(leaves, flowers, stems)
Dynasty XXI (ca. 1070–945 B.C.)
No measurements possible
ACC. 1-1d

Statuette of Thoth
(faience)
Late Period (ca. 664–332 B.C.)
Height 12.4 cm; width 3.1 cm; depth
  4.7 cm
ACC. 819-201

Brown Ware? Bowl
(ceramic)
Early Naqada I (ca. 3850–3750 B.C.)
Hu, U
Height 6.3 cm; diameter 11.6 cm
ACC. 1168-14

Small Red Ware Jar
(ceramic)
Early Naqada II (ca. 3650–3500 B.C.)
Hu, U
Height 12 cm; diameter 5.3 cm
ACC. 1168-16

Bag-shaped Rough Ware Jar
(ceramic)
Late Naqada I–early Naqada II (ca.
  3750–3500 B.C.)
Hu
Height 25.5 cm; diameter 6.7 cm
ACC. 1168-20

Shallow Rough Ware Bowl
(ceramic)
Naqada II (ca. 3650–3300 B.C.)
Hu, U
Height 7.2 cm; diameter 17.7 cm
ACC. 1168-23

Black-topped Red Ware Jar
(ceramic)
Naqada II (ca. 3650–3300 B.C.)
Hu, U73
Height 28.6 cm; diameter 11.4 cm
ACC. 1168-39

Decorated Ware Jar with Lugs
(ceramic, paint)
Naqada II (ca. 3650–3300 B.C.)
Hu, U105
Height 13.2 cm; diameter 12.3 cm
ACC. 1168-44

Wavy-Handled Ware Jar
(ceramic)
Late Naqada II (ca. 3550–3300 B.C.)
Hu, U177
Height 31.1 cm; diameter 11.7 cm
ACC. 1168-46

Black-topped Red Ware Bowl
(ceramic)
Naqada I (ca. 3850–3650 B.C.)
Hu, U197
Height 6.6 cm; diameter 16.7 cm
ACC. 1168-48

Late Ware Vase
(ceramic)
Naqada III (ca. 3300–3100 B.C.)
Hu, U302
Height 8.1 cm; diameter 6.5 cm
ACC. 1168-59

Red Polished Ware Bowl
(ceramic)
Early Naqada I (ca. 3850–3750 B.C.)
Hu, U398
Height 3.1 cm; diameter 7.9 cm
ACC. 1168-76

Black-topped Red Ware Bowl
(ceramic)
Late Naqada I (ca. 3750–3650 B.C.)
Hu
Height 15.8 cm; diameter 14.8 cm
ACC. 1168-77

Mug
(ceramic, paint)
Early Dynasty XVIII (ca. 1539–
  1425 B.C.)
Hu, W
Height 15.6 cm; diameter 6.6 cm
ACC. 1168-84

Decorated Ware Jar with Lugs
(ceramic, paint)
Naqada II (ca. 3650–3300 B.C.)
Hu, U57
Height 14 cm; diameter 12.2 cm
ACC. 1168-87

Decorated Jar with Wavy Lines
(ceramic, paint)
Naqada III–early Dynasty I
  (ca. 3300–3000 B.C.)
Hu, U87
Height 11 cm; diameter 7 cm
ACC. 1168-88

Nile Ware Jar
(ceramic)
Early Dynasty XVIII (ca. 1539–
  1425 B.C.)
Hu, D120

Height 32.1 cm; diameter 9.9 cm
ACC. 1168-92

Black-topped Red Ware Vase
(ceramic)
Late Naqada I (ca. 3750–3650 B.C.)
Hu, B241?
Height 15.8 cm; diameter 7.3 cm
ACC. 1168-98

Uninscribed Scarab
(chalcedony)
Dynasty XII–XIII (ca. 1979–1627/
  1606 B.C.)
Hu, Y414
Length 1.9 cm; width 1.4 cm
ACC. 1234-1

Scarab with Ankh *and* Neb *Signs*
(faience)
Late Middle Kingdom (ca. 1850–
  1627/1606 B.C.)
Hu, Y331
Length 1.4 cm; width 1 cm
ACC. 1234-12

Scarab with Ankhs *and Crown*
(glazed steatite)
Second Intermediate Period
  (ca. 1648–1539 B.C.)
Hu, Y53
Length 1.2 cm; width 0.8 cm
ACC. 1234-14

Lidded Kohl Pot
(calcite)
Dynasty XII–XIII (ca. 1979–1627/
  1606 B.C.)
Hu, Y51
Height 3.2 cm; diameter 4 cm
ACC. 1234-15

Necklace of Ovoid and Ball Beads
(carnelian, amethyst)
Dynasty XII–XIII (ca. 1979–1627/
  1606 B.C.)
Hu, Y51
Length 61 cm
ACC. 1234-23

Lump of Kohl
(manganese compound)
Dynasty XII (ca. 1979–1801 B.C.)
Hu
Diameter approx. 4.7 cm
ACC. 1234-24

Overseer Shabti
(faience)
Third Intermediate Period
  (ca. 1070–653 B.C.)
Abydos
Height 10.8 cm; width 3.7 cm
ACC. 1662-23

Ptah-Sokar Stamp Seal
(faience)
New Kingdom (ca. 1539–1070 B.C.)
Abydos, D28a
Height 3.6 cm; width 1.9 cm; depth
  1.7 cm
ACC. 1662-31

Pair of Penannular Earrings
(glass)
New Kingdom (ca. 1539–1070 B.C.)
Abydos, D28a
Diameter 2–2.1 cm; thickness 1.1–
  1.2 cm
ACC. 1662-33
ACC. 1662-33a

Anubis Amulet
(faience)
New Kingdom (ca. 1539–1070 B.C.)
Abydos, D28a
Height 2.4 cm; width 0.5 cm; depth
  1.1 cm
ACC. 1662-34

Amulet with Isis Nursing Infant Horus
(faience)
New Kingdom (ca. 1539–1070 B.C.)
Abydos, D28a
Height 2 cm; width 0.8 cm; depth
  1 cm
ACC. 1662-34a

Horus? as Falcon Amulet
(faience)
New Kingdom (ca. 1539–1070 B.C.)
Abydos, D28a
Height 1 cm; width 0.9 cm; depth
  1 cm
ACC. 1662-34b

Lidded Kohl Pot
(calcite, kohl)
New Kingdom (ca. 1539–1070 B.C.)
Abydos, D28a
Height 7.9 cm; diameter 6 cm
ACC. 1662-39

Multicolored Necklace of Cylinder Beads
(faience)
Second Intermediate Period–Dynasty
  XVIII (ca. 1648–1295 B.C.)
Abydos, D28a
Length 76.4 cm
ACC. 1662-45

Falcon Mummy
(animal remains, linen)
New Kingdom–Late Period
  (ca. 1539–332 B.C.)

Length 26.5 cm; width 8.4 cm
ACC. 1764-3a

Faked Cat Mummy
(padding, linen)
Roman Period (ca. 30 B.C.–A.D. 300)
Length 61.3 cm; width 10.2 cm
ACC. 1764-4b

Amulet of Shu
(faience)
Late Period (ca. 664–332 B.C.)
Height 3 cm; width 1.5 cm
ACC. 1867-8a

Fragments of Bracelet
(ivory)
Early Dynasty XVIII (ca. 1479–
  1425 B.C.)
Abydos, D116
No measurements possible
ACC. 1917-1a through h

Monkey Holding Kohl Tube
(limestone, paint)
Early Dynasty XVIII (ca. 1479–
  1425 B.C.)
Abydos, D116
Height 8.3 cm; width 2.4 cm; length
  5.5 cm
ACC. 1917-3
ACC. 1917-43 (lid)

Kohl Sticks
(bronze)
Early Dynasty XVIII (ca. 1479–
  1425 B.C.)
Abydos, D116
Length 15.5 cm; width 0.8 cm
ACC. 1917-5
Length 12.9 cm; width 0.6 cm
ACC. 1917-7

Ax
(bronze)
Early Dynasty XVIII (ca. 1479–
  1425 B.C.)
Abydos, D116
Length 14.1 cm; width 8.9 cm
ACC. 1917-11

Mirror with Handle Missing
(bronze)
Early Dynasty XVIII (ca. 1479–
  1425 B.C.)
Abydos, D116
Length 23.4 cm; width 20.5 cm
ACC. 1917-13

Cosmetic Spoon
(wood)
Early Dynasty XVIII (ca. 1479–
  1425 B.C.)
Abydos, D116
Length 7.4 cm; diameter 3.7 cm
ACC. 1917-16

Chisel
(bronze)
Early Dynasty XVIII (ca. 1479–
  1425 B.C.)
Abydos, D116
Length 5.2 cm; width 1.5 cm
ACC. 1917-18

Fastener
(bronze)
Early Dynasty XVIII (ca. 1479–
  1425 B.C.)
Abydos, D116
Length 6.6 cm; head width 1 cm
ACC. 1917-19

Piece of Pipe Stem Coral
(coral)
Early Dynasty XVIII (ca. 1479–
  1425 B.C.)
Abydos, D116
Length 2.6 cm; width 3.1 cm
ACC. 1917-22

Comb
(horn)
Early Dynasty XVIII (ca. 1479–
  1425 B.C.)
Abydos, D116
Length 7.3 cm; width 5 cm
ACC. 1917-24

Necklace with Amulets of Deities
(faience, carnelian)
Early Dynasty XVIII (ca. 1479–
  1425 B.C.)
Abydos, D116
Length 35.2 cm
ACC. 1917-31

Disk Beads
(freshwater shell)
Early Dynasty XVIII (ca. 1479–
  1425 B.C.)
Abydos, D116
Length 10.6 cm
ACC. 1917-33

Necklace with Leopard-Bead Spacer
(faience, gold, paste, calcite)
Early Dynasty XVIII (ca. 1479–
  1425 B.C.)
Abydos, D116
Length 78.4 cm
ACC. 1917-34

Necklace of Rosette-shaped Beads
(faience)
Early Dynasty XVIII (ca. 1479–
  1425 B.C.)
Abydos, D116
Length 29.6 cm
ACC. 1917-37

Necklace of Rosette-shaped Beads
(faience)
Early Dynasty XVIII (ca. 1479–
  1425 B.C.)
Abydos, D116
Length 27 cm
ACC. 1917-38

Amulet of Sekhmet
(faience)
Early Dynasty XVIII (ca. 1479–
  1425 B.C.)
Abydos, D116
Length 3.5 cm; width 0.8 cm
ACC. 1917-39

Amulet of Unknown Type
(faience)

Early Dynasty XVIII (ca. 1479–
  1425 B.C.)
Abydos, D116
Length 4.6 cm; width 1 cm
ACC. 1917-41

Fishhook
(bronze)
Early Dynasty XVIII (ca. 1479–
  1425 B.C.)
Abydos, D116
Length 3.7 cm; width 1.9 cm
ACC. 1917-44b

Piece of Lead
(lead)
Early Dynasty XVIII (ca. 1479–
  1425 B.C.)
Abydos, D116
Diameter 6.4 cm; thickness 0.5 cm
ACC. 1917-46

Ovoid Bead
(gold, paste)
Early Dynasty XVIII (ca. 1479–
  1425 B.C.)
Abydos, D116
Length 0.7 cm; diameter 0.35 cm
ACC. 1917-48

Pair of Leech-type Earrings
(gold, paste)
Early Dynasty XVIII (ca. 1479–
  1425 B.C.)
Abydos, D116
Length 1.6 cm; width 1.4 cm
ACC. 1917-49
ACC. 1917-50

Bowl
(bronze)
Early Dynasty XVIII (ca. 1479–
  1425 B.C.)
Abydos, D116
Height 3.9 cm; diameter 15.5 cm
ACC. 1917-53

Lumps of Kohl
(galena)
Early Dynasty XVIII (ca. 1479–
  1425 B.C.)
Abydos, D116
No measurements possible
ACC. 1917-55

Necklace with Cowrie Shells
(faience, marine shell)
Early Dynasty XVIII (ca. 1479–
  1425 B.C.)
Abydos, D116
Length 35 cm
ACC. 1917-56

Scarab with Geometric Design
(glazed steatite)
Early Dynasty XVIII (ca. 1479–
  1425 B.C.)
Abydos, D116
Length 1.4 cm; width 1 cm
ACC. 1917-57

*Duck-shaped Amulet with Menkheperre's
  Cartouche*
(faience)

Early Dynasty XVIII (ca. 1479– 1425 B.C.)
Abydos, D116
Length 1.2 cm; width 0.8 cm
ACC. 1917-58

Plaque with Menkheperre's Cartouche
(faience)
Early Dynasty XVIII (ca. 1479– 1425 B.C.)
Abydos, D116
Length 1.6 cm; width 1.2
ACC. 1917-64

Scarab with Lion and Scorpion
(faience)
Early Dynasty XVIII (ca. 1479– 1425 B.C.)
Abydos, D116
Length 1.6 cm; width 1.1 cm
ACC. 1917-66

Scarab Depicting Standing Pharaoh
(faience)
Early Dynasty XVIII (ca. 1479– 1425 B.C.)
Abydos, D116
Length 1.8 cm; width 1.3 cm
ACC. 1917-67

Scarab with Amun-Re's Name
(faience)
Early Dynasty XVIII (ca. 1479– 1425 B.C.)
Abydos, D116
Length 1.8 cm; width 1.3 cm
ACC. 1917-68

Scarab with Menkheperre's Cartouche
(faience)
Early Dynasty XVIII (ca. 1479– 1425 B.C.)
Abydos, D116
Length 1.5 cm; width 1 cm
ACC. 1917-69

Scarab with Amun-Re's Name
(faience)
Early Dynasty XVIII (ca. 1479– 1425 B.C.)
Abydos, D116
Length 0.9 cm; width 0.7
ACC. 1917-70

Cowroid with Glyphs
(faience)
Early Dynasty XVIII (ca. 1479– 1425 B.C.)
Abydos, D116
Length 0.6 cm; width 0.8 cm
ACC. 1917-71

Scarab with Floral Design
(faience)
Early Dynasty XVIII (ca. 1479– 1425 B.C.)
Abydos, D116
Length 1 cm; width 0.8 cm
ACC. 1917-72

Scarab with Menkheperre's Cartouche
(faience)
Early Dynasty XVIII (ca. 1479– 1425 B.C.)
Abydos, D116

Length 1.1 cm; width 0.8 cm
ACC. 1917-74

Scarab with Cartouche?
(unglazed steatite)
Early Dynasty XVIII (ca. 1479– 1425 B.C.)
Abydos, D116
Length 1.3 cm; width 0.9 cm
ACC. 1917-75

Scarab with Scorpion and Nefer *Sign*
(faience)
Early Dynasty XVIII (ca. 1479– 1425 B.C.)
Abydos, D116
Length 1.2 cm; width 0.9 cm
ACC. 1917-76

Scarab with Taweret?
(faience)
Early Dynasty XVIII (ca. 1479– 1425 B.C.)
Abydos, D116
Length 0.8 cm; width 0.6 cm
ACC. 1917-77

Scarab with Checkerboard Design
(faience)
Early Dynasty XVIII (ca. 1479– 1425 B.C.)
Abydos, D116
Length 1.6 cm; width 1.4 cm
ACC. 1917-79

Scarab with Monkey Holding Nefer
(faience)
Early Dynasty XVIII (ca. 1479– 1425 B.C.)
Abydos, D116
Length 1.5 cm; width 1.1 cm
ACC. 1917-80

Kohl Jar
(calcite)
Early Dynasty XVIII (ca. 1479– 1425 B.C.)
Abydos, D116
Height 5.5 cm; diameter 4.8 cm
ACC. 1917-83

Double Bilbil
(ceramic)
Second Intermediate Period–Dynasty XVIII (ca. 1648–1295 B.C.)
Abydos, D64b
Height 10.1 cm; width of pair 6.9 cm
ACC. 1917-94

Scarab with Hieroglyphs
(faience)
Second Intermediate Period–early Dynasty XVIII (ca. 1648–1425 B.C.)
Abydos, D64b
Length 2 cm; width 1.4 cm
ACC. 1917-95

Kohl Stick
(bronze)
Second Intermediate Period–early Dynasty XVIII (ca. 1648–1425 B.C.)
Abydos, D64b
Length 9.7 cm; diameter 0.6 cm
ACC. 1917-97

Small Jar
(calcite)
Dynasty XIII–XVII (ca. 1801– 1539 B.C.)
Abydos, D92
Height 6.8 cm; diameter 6.1 cm
ACC. 1917-99

Necklace of Small Disk Beads
(faience, calcite)
Dynasty XIII–XVII (ca. 1801– 1539 B.C.)
Abydos, D92
Length 44 cm
ACC. 1917-104

Decorative Overlay from Box
(bone, paste)
Second Intermediate Period–early Dynasty XVIII (ca. 1648–1425 B.C.)
Abydos, D66
Length 5.1–12.1 cm; width 1.2– 2.2 cm
ACC. 1917-108
ACC. 1917-110
ACC. 1917-112
ACC. 1917-115
ACC. 1917-120
ACC. 1917-121
ACC. 1917-122
ACC. 1917-129

Kohl Pot in Three Parts
(gabbro)
Second Intermediate Period–early Dynasty XVIII (ca. 1648–1425 B.C.)
Abydos, D66
Height 5.3 cm; diameter 4.4 cm
ACC. 1917-134

Kohl Pot with Lid
(steatite)
Dynasty XII–XIII (ca. 1979–1627/ 1606 B.C.)
Abydos, D66
Height 2.7 cm; diameter 4.4 cm
ACC. 1917-135

Necklace with Bes Amulet
(carnelian, bone, faience?, granite)
Early Dynasty XVIII (ca. 1479– 1425 B.C.)
Abydos, D102?
Length 41.4 cm
ACC. 1917-139

Disk Beads
(glass)
Second Intermediate Period–early Dynasty XVIII (ca. 1648–1425 B.C.)
Abydos, D66
Length 19.2 cm
ACC. 1917-140

Necklace with Amulets
(carnelian, faience, glass, amazonite)
Second Intermediate Period–early Dynasty XVIII (ca. 1648–1425 B.C.)
Abydos, D66
Length 71 cm
ACC. 1917-143

Necklace of Graduated Ball Beads
(carnelian, glass, electrum)

Early Dynasty XVIII (ca. 1479– 1425 B.C.)
Abydos, D102
Length 68.5 cm
ACC. 1917-145

Necklace with Amulets
(carnelian, electrum)
Second Intermediate Period–early Dynasty XVIII (ca. 1648–1425 B.C.)
Abydos, D66
Length 61.8 cm
ACC. 1917-146

Pair of Penannular Earrings
(gold)
Early Dynasty XVIII (ca. 1479– 1425 B.C.)
Abydos, D102
Approx. diameter 2.5 cm; thickness 1 cm
ACC. 1917-148
ACC. 1917-149

Pair of Penannular Earrings
(gold)
Early Dynasty XVIII (ca. 1479– 1425 B.C.)
Abydos, D102
Diameter 2.2–2.3 cm; thickness 0.8– 0.9 cm
ACC. 1917-150
ACC. 1917-151

Wig Ornaments?
(electrum?)
Early Dynasty XVIII (ca. 1479– 1425 B.C.)
Abydos, D102
Width 2–2.5 cm; diameter 0.7– 0.8 cm.
ACC. 1917-157
ACC. 1917-158

Scarab Ring
(faience, bronze)
Second Intermediate Period–early Dynasty XVIII (ca. 1648–1425 B.C.)
Abydos, D102
Length 1.8 cm; width 1.1 cm
ACC. 1917-159

Footed Bowl
(Egyptian blue)
Early Dynasty XVIII (ca. 1479– 1425 B.C.)
Abydos, D102
Height (incomplete) 3.1 cm; diameter 7.9 cm
ACC. 1917-162

Polishing Stone
(quartz)
Early Dynasty XVIII (ca. 1479– 1425 B.C.)
Abydos, D102
Length 10.6 cm; width 5.3 cm
ACC. 1917-165

Weight
(sandstone)
Early Dynasty XVIII (ca. 1479– 1425 B.C.)
Abydos, D102

Length 4.4 cm; width 4.6 cm;
thickness 3.4 cm
ACC. 1917-167

Scarab Bezel
(carnelian, gold)
Early Dynasty XVIII (ca. 1479–
1425 B.C.)
Abydos, D102
Length 2.2 cm; width 1.6 cm
ACC. 1917-177

Scarab with Flower Motif
(faience)
Early Dynasty XVIII (ca. 1479–
1425 B.C.)
Abydos, D116
Length 1.4 cm; width 1.1 cm
ACC. 1917-184

Scarab
(steatite)
Second Intermediate Period–early
Dynasty XVIII (ca. 1648–1425 B.C.)
Abydos, D102
Length 1.6 cm; width 1 cm
ACC. 1917-185

Scarab with Menkheperre's Cartouche
(faience)
Early Dynasty XVIII (ca. 1479–
1425 B.C.)
Abydos, D102
Length 0.9 cm; width 0.6 cm
ACC. 1917-191

Scarab Bearing Aakheperkare's Cartouche
(faience)
Early Dynasty XVIII (ca. 1493–
1481 B.C.)
Abydos, D102
Length 1 cm; width 0.8 cm
ACC. 1917-192

Design Amulet Bearing Princess Neferure's Name
(glass)
Early Dynasty XVIII (ca. 1481–
1468 B.C.)
Abydos, D102
Length 0.9 cm; width 0.7 cm
ACC. 1917-201

Amulet with Duck-shaped Back
(faience)
Early Dynasty XVIII (ca. 1479–
1425 B.C.)
Abydos, D102
Length 1 cm; width 0.7 cm
ACC. 1917-203

Plaque with Pharaoh and Three Deities
(glazed steatite)
Early Dynasty XVIII (ca. 1479–
1425 B.C.)
Abydos, D102
Length 1.4 cm; width 1 cm
ACC. 1917-208

Cowroid Inscribed with Amun-Re's Name
(faience)
Early Dynasty XVIII (ca. 1479–
1425 B.C.)
Abydos, D102
Length 1.4 cm; width 0.9 cm
ACC. 1917-213

Bead Inscribed with Djeserkare's Cartouche
(glass)
Early Dynasty XVIII (ca. 1514–
1493 B.C.)
Abydos, D102
Length 1.7 cm; diameter 0.9 cm
ACC. 1917-217

Pair of Inlaid Eyes for Coffin
(steatite)
Early Dynasty XVIII (ca. 1479–
1425 B.C.)
Abydos, D119
Approx.: length 1.4 cm; width 3 cm
ACC. 1917-222 (right)
ACC. 1917-223 (left)

Ferrule
(bronze)
Early Dynasty XVIII (ca. 1479–
1425 B.C.)
Abydos, D119
Length 10 cm; diameter 3 cm
ACC. 1917-227

Whetstone
(sandstone)
Early Dynasty XVIII (ca. 1479–
1425 B.C.)
Abydos, D119
Length 6.6 cm; width 1.8 cm
ACC. 1917-229

Tweezers
(bronze)
Early Dynasty XVIII (ca. 1479–
1425 B.C.)
Abydos, D119
Length 3.9 cm; width 1.3 cm
ACC. 1917-230

Model Face for Mummy
(plaster, paint)
Early Dynasty XVIII (ca. 1479–
1425 B.C.)
Abydos, D119
Height 5.8 cm; width 5 cm; thickness
2.9 cm
ACC. 1917-232

Monkey Holding Kohl Tube
(fine-grained sandstone, paint)
Early Dynasty XVIII (ca. 1479–
1425 B.C.)
Abydos, D119
Height 5.6 cm; width 4.2 cm; depth
2.2 cm
ACC. 1917-235

Kohl Jar
(limestone, paint)
Early Dynasty XVIII (ca. 1479–
1425 B.C.)
Abydos, D119
Height 7.2 cm; diameter 6.1 cm
ACC. 1917-236

Net Sinkers?
(lead)
Early Dynasty XVIII (ca. 1479–
1425 B.C.)
Abydos, D119
Length 1.9–2.2 cm; width 0.7–
1.5 cm

ACC. 1917-237
ACC. 1917-238
ACC. 1917-239

Scarab Depicting Djed-*Pillars*
(glazed steatite)
Early Dynasty XVIII (ca. 1479–
1425 B.C.)
Abydos, D119
Length 1.6 cm; width 1.1 cm
ACC. 1917-257

Ball and Circular Beads
(faience)
Dynasty XII (ca. 1979–1801 B.C.)
Abydos, D73
Length 33 cm
ACC. 1917-266

Lion-shaped Design Amulet
(glazed steatite, gold)
Second Intermediate Period
(ca. 1648–1539 B.C.)
Abydos, D71
Height 1.6 cm; width 1.3 cm; length
2.3 cm
ACC. 1917-267

Fly Amulet
(faience)
Second Intermediate Period
(ca. 1648–1539 B.C.)
Abydos, D71
Length 1.5 cm; width 0.8 cm
ACC. 1917-269

Pin
(bronze)
Second Intermediate Period
(ca. 1648–1539 B.C.)
Abydos, D71
Length 7.8 cm; head width 0.7 cm
ACC. 1917-274

Bowl with Lotus Design
(faience)
Early Dynasty XVIII (ca. 1479–
1425 B.C.)
Abydos, D111
Height 3.3 cm; diameter 13.6 cm
ACC. 1917-279

Wig Ornament?
(bronze)
Second Intermediate Period–early
Dynasty XVIII (ca. 1648–1425 B.C.)
Abydos, D87
Diameter 1.6 cm; thickness 1.7 cm
ACC. 1917-313

Wig Ornament?
(bronze, gold)
Second Intermediate Period–early
Dynasty XVIII (ca. 1648–1425 B.C.)
Abydos, D87
Diameter 1.3 cm; thickness 0.8 cm
ACC. 1917-314

Tweezers
(bronze)
Second Intermediate Period–early
Dynasty XVIII (ca. 1648–1425 B.C.)
Abydos, D87
Length 3.6 cm; width 0.6 cm
ACC. 1917-321

Double Bag-shaped Jar
(calcite)
Early Dynasty XVIII (ca. 1479–
1425 B.C.)
Abydos, D64a
Height 5.5 cm; width of pair 5.3 cm
ACC. 1917-322

Kohl Stick
(hematite)
Early Dynasty XVIII (ca. 1479–
1425 B.C.)
Abydos, D64a
Length 6.4 cm; width 0.5 cm
ACC. 1917-325

Lidded Kohl Pot
(calcite)
Early Dynasty XVIII (ca. 1479–
1425 B.C.)
Abydos, D64a
Height 6.9 cm; diameter 6.6 cm
ACC. 1917-330

Footed Ointment Jar
(calcite)
Early Dynasty XVIII, reign of
Tuthmosis III (ca. 1479–1425 B.C.)
Abydos, D102
Height 8 cm; width 5.2 cm
ACC. 1917-335

Box Fragment Inscribed for King Den
(burnt ivory)
Mid Dynasty I (ca. 3000 B.C.)
Abydos, tomb of Den
Length 5.6 cm; width 2.8 cm; thick-
ness 1 cm
ACC. 1917-336

Needles
(copper)
Early Dynastic Period (ca. 3100–
2750 B.C.)
Abydos, Umm el-Qaab
Length 4.3–8.2 cm; width 0.1–
0.3 cm
ACC. 1917-337a through d

Chisels
(copper)
Mid Dynasty I (ca. 3000 B.C.)
Tombs of Djer and Den
Length 7.9–11.7 cm; width 0.4–
1.3 cm
ACC. 1917-343 (Djer)
ACC. 1917-531 (Den)
ACC. 1917-532 (Den)

Inlay for Furniture?
(ivory, paste)
Mid Dynasty I (ca. 3000 B.C.)
Abydos, tomb of Den
Length 1.2 cm; width 0.5 cm
ACC. 1917-369

Shallow Bowl
(ceramic)
Early Dynasty XVIII (ca. 1479–
1425 B.C.)
Abydos, D102
Height 7.1 cm; diameter 26 cm
ACC. 1917-377

Carinated Jar
(ceramic, paint)

Early Dynasty XVIII (ca. 1479–
   1425 B.C.)
Abydos, D102
Height 10.5 cm; diameter 6.8 cm
ACC. 1917-379

Carinated Jar
(ceramic, paint)
Early Dynasty XVIII (ca. 1479–
   1425 B.C.)
Abydos, D102
Height 10.8 cm; diameter 8.4 cm
ACC. 1917-379a

Shallow Bowl
(ceramic, paint)
Early Dynasty XVIII (ca. 1479–
   1425 B.C.)
Abydos, D102
Height 7.1 cm; diameter 17.6 cm
ACC. 1917-380

Mug
(ceramic)
Early Dynasty XVIII (ca. 1479–
   1425 B.C.)
Abydos, D102
Height 8 cm; diameter 3.1 cm
ACC. 1917-381

Large Bag-shaped Jar
(ceramic)
Early Dynasty XVIII (ca. 1479–
   1425 B.C.)
Abydos, D102
Height 27.2 cm; diameter 4.7 cm
ACC. 1917-382

Mug
(ceramic, paint)
Early Dynasty XVIII (ca. 1479–
   1425 B.C.)
Abydos, D102
Height 14.3 cm; diameter 4.6 cm
ACC. 1917-383

Large Bowl
(ceramic)
Early Dynasty XVIII (ca. 1479–
   1425 B.C.)
Abydos, D102
Height 13.2 cm; diameter 26 cm
ACC. 1917-386

Cylinder Vase
(travertine calcite)
Early Dynasty I (ca. 3050 B.C.)
Abydos, tomb of Djer
Height 27.3 cm; width 16.3 cm
ACC. 1917-388

Unfinished Cylinder Vase
(limestone)
Late Dynasty II (ca. 2750 B.C.)
Abydos, tomb of Kha'sekhemwy
Height 14.3 cm; diameter 10.4 cm
ACC. 1917-390

Unfinished Cylinder Vase
(limestone)
Late Dynasty II (ca. 2750 B.C.)
Abydos, tomb of Kha'sekhemwy
Height 18.6 cm; diameter 10.8 cm
ACC. 1917-390a

Small Bowl with Handle
(calcite)

Early Dynasty XVIII (ca. 1479–
   1425 B.C.)
Abydos, D119
Height 7 cm; diameter 8.6 cm
ACC. 1917-391

Bag-shaped Jar
(calcite)
Early Dynasty XVIII (ca. 1479–
   1425 B.C.)
Abydos, D119
Height 14.9 cm; diameter 8.8 cm
ACC. 1917-392

Amphora
(calcite)
Early Dynasty XVIII (ca. 1479–
   1425 B.C.)
Abydos, D119
Height 16.1 cm; diameter 5.4 cm
ACC. 1917-393

Small Lugged Jar
(mud, paint)
Early Dynasty XVIII (ca. 1479–
   1425 B.C.)
Abydos, D116
Height 9.9 cm; diameter 3.6 cm
ACC. 1917-402

"Pilgrim Flask"
(ceramic, paint)
Early Dynasty XVIII (ca. 1479–
   1425 B.C.)
Abydos, D116
Height 8.3 cm; diameter 2 cm
ACC. 1917-406

Stopper for Small Jar
(mud)
Early Dynasty XVIII (ca. 1479–
   1425 B.C.)
Abydos, D116
Height 9 cm; diameter 3.6 cm
ACC. 1917-409

Arrowheads
(ivory)
Mid Dynasty I (ca. 3050 B.C.)
Abydos, tomb of Djer
Approx. length 7.5 cm; width 0.6 cm
ACC. 1917-435
ACC. 1917-437

Uninscribed Label
(ivory)
Early Dynasty I (ca. 3100 B.C.)
Abydos, B16
Length 1.6 cm; width 1.2 cm
ACC. 1917-443

Mirror? Handle
(ivory)
Early Dynasty I (ca. 3100 B.C.)
Abydos, B14
Length 6 cm; width 2 cm
ACC. 1917-446

Model Harpoon
(copper)
Late Dynasty II (ca. 2750 B.C.)
Abydos, tomb of Kha'sekhemwy
Length 9.7 cm; width 1 cm
ACC. 1917-450

Model Ax
(copper)

Late Dynasty II (ca. 2750 B.C.)
Abydos, tomb of Kha'sekhemwy
Length 9 cm; width 9.1 cm
ACC. 1917-456

Model Adze
(copper)
Late Dynasty II (ca. 2750 B.C.)
Abydos, tomb of Kha'sekhemwy
Length 10.1 cm; width 3.6 cm
ACC. 1917-457

Chisel
(copper)
Late Dynasty II (ca. 2750 B.C.)
Abydos, tomb of Kha'sekhemwy
Length 8.7 cm; width 2.1 cm
ACC. 1917-458

Fishhooks
(bronze)
Early Dynasty XVIII (ca. 1479–
   1425 B.C.)
Abydos, D102?
Length 2.1–3.2 cm; width 1–1.3 cm
ACC. 1917-462
ACC. 1917-463
ACC. 1917-464

Small Lugged Jar
(ceramic)
Early Dynasty XVIII (ca. 1479–
   1425 B.C.)?
Abydos, D116
Height 11 cm; diameter 5.7 cm
ACC. 1917-475

Footed Ointment Jar
(Egyptian blue)
Early Dynasty XVIII (ca. 1479–
   1425 B.C.)
Abydos, D116
Height 8.7 cm; diameter 7 cm
ACC. 1917-476

Small Carinated Jar
(ceramic)
Early Dynasty XVIII (ca. 1479–
   1425 B.C.)
Abydos, D116
Height 6.5 cm; diameter 5.8 cm
ACC. 1917-477

Lamp
(ceramic)
Third Intermediate–Late Periods
   (ca. 1070–332 B.C.)
Abydos, D116
Height 7.4 cm; diameter 9.9 cm
ACC. 1917-478

Jug with Polished Surface
(ceramic)
Early Dynasty XVIII (ca. 1479–
   1425 B.C.)
Abydos, D119
Height 19.4 cm; diameter 7.9 cm
ACC. 1917-492

Small Bowl
(ceramic, paint)
Second Intermediate Period–early
   Dynasty XVIII (ca. 1648–1425 B.C.)
Abydos, D87
Height 6.6 cm; diameter 10 cm
ACC. 1917-493

Cylinder Vase Inscribed with Serekh of Qa
(ceramic, ink)
Late Naqada III (ca. 3150–3100 B.C.)
Abydos, B7, tomb of Qa
Height (incomplete) 20.9 cm; diam-
   eter 9.9 cm
ACC. 1917-495

Shallow Bowl
(ceramic)
Early Dynasty XVIII (ca. 1479–
   1425 B.C.)
Abydos, D102
Height 7.6 cm; diameter 25.2 cm
ACC. 1917-497

Shallow Bowl
(ceramic)
Early Dynasty XVIII (ca. 1479–
   1425 B.C.)
Abydos, D102
Height 8 cm; diameter 27.6 cm
ACC. 1917-498

Shallow Bowl
(ceramic)
Early Dynasty XVIII (ca. 1479–
   1425 B.C.)
Abydos, D102
Height 8.2 cm; diameter 27.1 cm
ACC. 1917-499

Carinated Jar
(ceramic, paint)
Early Dynasty XVIII (ca. 1479–
   1425 B.C.)
Abydos, D102
Height 11.7 cm; diameter 8 cm
ACC. 1917-501

Carinated Jar
(ceramic, paint)
Early Dynasty XVIII (ca. 1479–
   1425 B.C.)
Abydos, D102
Height 6.8 cm; diameter 4.5 cm
ACC. 1917-502

Mug
(ceramic)
Early Dynasty XVIII (ca. 1479–
   1425 B.C.)
Abydos, D102
Height 14.2 cm; diameter 4.8 cm
ACC. 1917-503

Carinated Jar
(ceramic)
Early Dynasty XVIII (ca. 1479–
   1425 B.C.)
Abydos, D102
Height 10.1 cm; diameter 6.7 cm
ACC. 1917-505

Carinated Jar
(ceramic, paint)
Early Dynasty XVIII (ca. 1479–
   1425 B.C.)
Abydos, D102
Height 10 cm; diameter 7.2 cm
ACC. 1917-506

Carinated Jar
(ceramic, paint)
Early Dynasty XVIII (ca. 1479–
   1425 B.C.)

Abydos, D102
Height 4.6 cm; diameter 3.5 cm
ACC. 1917-507

Carinated Jar
(ceramic, paint)
Early Dynasty XVIII (ca. 1479–
  1425 B.C.)
Abydos, D102
Height 9.5 cm; diameter 6.2 cm
ACC. 1917-508

Carinated Jar
(ceramic, paint)
Early Dynasty XVIII (ca. 1479–
  1425 B.C.)
Abydos, D116
Height 8 cm; diameter 5.5 cm
ACC. 1917-509

Carinated Jar
(ceramic, paint)
Early Dynasty XVIII (ca. 1479–
  1425 B.C.)
Abydos, D102
Height 7.7 cm; diameter 5.5 cm
ACC. 1917-510

Mug
(ceramic)
Early Dynasty XVIII (ca. 1479–
  1425 B.C.)
Abydos, D102
Height 16.5 cm; diameter 5 cm
ACC. 1917-511

Small Carinated Jar
(ceramic, paint)
Early Dynasty XVIII (ca. 1479–
  1425 B.C.)
Abydos, D102
Height 11.2 cm; diameter 7.2 cm
ACC. 1917-513

Jar
(ceramic, paint)
Early Dynasty XVIII (ca. 1479–
  1425 B.C.)
Abydos, D102
Height 20.4 cm; diameter 6.3 cm
ACC. 1917-515

Carinated Jar
(ceramic, paint)
Early Dynasty XVIII (ca. 1479–
  1425 B.C.)
Abydos, D102
Height 10.7 cm; diameter 7.3 cm
ACC. 1917-517

Large Carinated Jar
(ceramic, paint)
Early Dynasty XVIII (ca. 1479–
  1425 B.C.)
Abydos, D102
Height 17.5 cm; diameter 10 cm
ACC. 1917-518

Carinated Jar
(ceramic, paint)
Early Dynasty XVIII (ca. 1479–
  1425 B.C.)
Abydos, D102
Height 9.3 cm; diameter 7.4 cm
ACC. 1917-520

Small Bowl
(ceramic)
Early Dynasty XVIII (ca. 1479–
  1425 B.C.)
Abydos, D102
Height 6.5 cm; diameter 11.6 cm
ACC. 1917-522

Carinated Bowl
(ceramic, paint)
Early Dynasty XVIII (ca. 1479–
  1425 B.C.)
Abydos, D102
Height 4.9 cm; diameter 14 cm
ACC. 1917-523

Small Jar
(ceramic, paint)
Early Dynasty XVIII (ca. 1479–
  1425 B.C.)
Abydos, D102
Height 6.1 cm; diameter 5.3 cm
ACC. 1917-524

Carinated Jar
(ceramic)
Early Dynasty XVIII (ca. 1479–
  1425 B.C.)
Abydos, D102
Height 8.3 cm; diameter 6.6 cm
ACC. 1917-526

Large Bowl
(ceramic, paint)
Early Dynasty XVIII (ca. 1539–
  1425 B.C.)
Abydos, D111
Height 7.9 cm; diameter 25.8 cm
ACC. 1917-530

Bag-shaped Jar
(ceramic, paint)
Early Dynasty XVIII (ca. 1479–
  1425 B.C.)
Abydos, D102
Height 26 cm; diameter 10.1 cm
ACC. 1917-533

Small Ointment Jar
(faience)
Early Dynasty XVIII (ca. 1479–
  1425 B.C.)
Abydos, D116
Height 5.8 cm; diameter 3.9 cm
ACC. 1917-535

Game Piece with Bes-Image
(faience)
Early Dynasty XVIII (ca. 1479–
  1425 B.C.)
Abydos, D116
Height 1.2 cm; diameter 1.4 cm
ACC. 1917-538

Pen
(reed)
Ptolemaic Period (ca. 332–30 B.C.)
Faiyum
Length 9.2 cm; width 0.9
ACC. 1948-5

Incised Fragment from Bowl
(calcite)
New Kingdom (ca. 1539–1070 B.C.)
Faiyum

Height 4.7 cm; width 5 cm
ACC. 1948-8

Mummy Tag
(wood, paint)
Mid to late Roman Period (ca. A.D.
  100–395)?
Faiyum
Length 11.9 cm; width 5.9 cm
ACC. 1948-10

Waxed Writing Board
(wood, wax)
Late Ptolemaic–mid Roman Periods
  (ca. 50 B.C.–A.D. 250)
Umm el-'Atl
Length 11.4 cm; width 20 cm; thick-
  ness 0.6 cm
ACC. 1948-19

Handle to Metal Jar?
(bronze, lead)
Ptolemaic Period (ca. 332–30 B.C.)
Faiyum
Length 11.5 cm; width 4.7 cm
ACC. 1948-41

Statuette of Serapis
(wood)
Ptolemaic–Roman Periods (ca. 310/
  305 B.C.–A.D. 395)
Harit, H286
Height 20.7 cm; width 11 cm; depth
  5.9 cm
ACC. 1948-44

Child's Bracelet?
(bronze)
Roman Period (ca. 30 B.C.–A.D. 395)
Qasr el-Banât
Diameter 4.3 cm; thickness 0.8 cm
ACC. 1948-47

Decorated Ball
(faience)
Mid to late Dynasty XVIII (ca. 1450–
  1295 B.C.)
Deir el-Bahri
Diameter 3.8 cm; thickness 3.4 cm
ACC. 1948-49

Model Cow's Head
(faience)
Mid to late Dynasty XVIII (ca. 1450–
  1295 B.C.)
Deir el-Bahri
Length 1.8 cm; width 1.3 cm
ACC. 1948-50

Cartouche-shaped Amulet
(faience)
Dynasty XVIII, probably reign of
  Tuthmosis III (ca. 1479–1425 B.C.)
Deir el-Bahri
Length 2.1 cm; width 1.1 cm
ACC. 1948-51

Mixed Beads
(faience)
Dynasty XVIII (ca. 1539–1295 B.C.)
Deir el-Bahri
Length 48 cm
ACC. 1948-52

Fish-shaped Cosmetic Palette
(slate)

Naqada II (ca. 3650–3300 B.C.)
Naqada/Hu, B21
Length 13.9 cm; width 10.4 cm
ACC. 1948-55

Round Cosmetic Palette
(slate)
Late Naqada III (ca. 3100 B.C.)
Naqada or Hu
Diameter 11.2 cm; thickness 1.6 cm
ACC. 1948-56

Rectangular Cosmetic Palette
(slate)
Naqada III (ca. 3300–3100 B.C.)
Naqada or Hu
Length 11 cm; width 7.8 cm
ACC. 1948-57

Coin of Nero
(bronze)
Early Roman Period (A.D. 54–68)
Umm el-'Atl, R183
Diameter 2.4 cm; thickness 0.45 cm
ACC. 1948-59b5

Coin of Hadrian
(bronze)
Mid Roman Period (A.D. 117–138)
Umm el-'Atl, R183
Diameter 2.7 cm; thickness 0.4 cm
ACC. 1948-59h3

Serrated Blade
(flint)
Neolithic, Faiyum A (ca. 5450–
  3850 B.C.)
Length 7.6 cm; width 2.4 cm
ACC. 2049-519

Shouldered Jar
(ceramic)
Dynasty VI–VIII (ca. 2423–
  2213 B.C.)
Height 18.5 cm; diameter 6.9 cm
ACC. 2049-521

*Lintel of "Administrator of the Ruler's
  Table," Sebekhotep*
(limestone)
Dynasty XII–XIII (ca. 1979–1627/
  1606 B.C.)
Abydos, Cemetery D
Length 28.4 cm; width 23 cm; thick-
  ness 10.1 cm
ACC. 2231-4

Ostracon with Cartouche of Ramesses II
(limestone, ink)
Dynasty XIX, reign of Ramesses II
  (ca. 1279–1213 B.C.)
Abydos, Osiris temple
Length 17.5 cm; width 12.3 cm
ACC. 2231-5

Jackal-headed Lid for Shabti *Jar*
(ceramic)
Dynasty XIX–XX (ca. 1295–
  1070 B.C.)
Abydos, Cemetery G?
Height 7.6 cm; diameter 10.5 cm
ACC. 2231-6

Uninscribed Shabti
(ceramic)

Dynasty XXX–XXXI (ca. 380–332 B.C.)
Abydos
Length 15.4 cm; width 3.6 cm
ACC. 2231-7a

Long-necked Jar
(ceramic)
Ptolemaic Period (ca. 332–30 B.C.)
Abydos, T7
Height 12.2 cm; diameter 2.5 cm
ACC. 2231-8c

Bottle
(ceramic)
Late Dynasty XVIII (ca. 1390–1295 B.C.)
Abydos, Cemetery G?
Height 22.6 cm; diameter 1.5 cm
ACC. 2231-8e

Partial Set of Shabtis
(faience)
Ptolemaic Period (ca. 332–30 B.C.)
Abydos, Cemetery G
Height 9.9–10.3 cm; width 3–3.4 cm
ACC. 2231-9
ACC. 2231-9f
ACC. 2231-9g
ACC. 2231-9m
ACC. 2231-9o
ACC. 2231-9q
ACC. 2231-9r

Juvenile Crocodile Mummy
(animal remains, dyed linen)
Roman Period (ca. 30 B.C.–A.D. 300)
Abydos
Length 45 cm; width 7.1 cm; thickness 6.3 cm
ACC. 2231-11

Spindle Whorl
(limestone)
Early Dynastic Period (ca. 3100–2750 B.C.)
Abydos, Osiris temenos
Height 2 cm; diameter 3.2 cm
ACC. 2231-13

Cylinder Beads
(faience)
Dynasty I (ca. 3100–2900 B.C.)
Abydos, Osiris temenos?
Length 119 cm
ACC. 2231-14

Model? Jar
(indurated limestone)
Dynasty I (ca. 3100–2900 B.C.)
Abydos, M26-5, Osiris temenos
Height 3.8 cm; diameter 5.3 cm
ACC. 2231-16

Model? Bowl
(breccia)
Dynasty I (ca. 3100–2900 B.C.)
Abydos, M26-6, Osiris temenos
Height 2.8 cm; diameter 5.3 cm
ACC. 2231-16a

Cylinder Bead Necklace
(steatite)
Dynasty I (ca. 3100–2900 B.C.)
Abydos, probably Osiris temenos

Each bead approx.: length 1 cm; diameter 0.6 cm
ACC. 2231-16c

Spindle Whorl
(glass)
Ptolemaic–Roman Periods (ca. 332 B.C.–A.D. 300)
Faiyum
Height 0.7 cm; diameter 2.5 cm
ACC. 2231-26i

Cosmetic Box Decorated with Nucleated Circles
(wood, paste)
Roman Period (ca. 30 B.C.–A.D. 395)
Faiyum
Length 7.2 cm; width 7 cm; height 5.2 cm
ACC. 2231-27

Beads
(glass)
Ptolemaic–Roman Periods (ca. 332 B.C.–A.D. 395)
Faiyum
Length 28 cm
ACC. 2231-28

Necklace with Tassels
(faience)
New Kingdom (ca. 1539–1070 B.C.)
Abydos?
Length 69 cm
ACC. 2231-29

Scarab Depicting Pharaoh
(faience)
New Kingdom (ca. 1539–1070 B.C.)
Abydos?
Length 1.1 cm; width 0.8 cm
ACC. 2231-31

Osiris Statuette
(bronze)
Dynasty XXVI (ca. 664–525 B.C.)
Abydos, Osiris temple
Height 20.4 cm; width 5.9 cm
ACC. 2400-2a

Necklace of Cylinder Beads
(faience)
Dynasty XVIII (ca. 1539–1295 B.C.)
Abydos, Osiris temenos
Length 47 cm
ACC. 2400-6

Anubis Statuette
(wood)
Ptolemaic Period (ca. 332–30 B.C.)
Hiba
Height 9 cm; width 4.6 cm; length 19 cm
ACC. 2400-13

Bracelet
(bronze)
Post-Pharaonic Period (ca. A.D. 395–700)
Hiba
Diameter 4 cm; thickness 0.4 cm
ACC. 2400-14b

Disk Beads
(faience)
Dynasty XXVII (ca. 525–404/401 B.C.)?

Hiba
Length 40.7 cm
ACC. 2400-17

Spindle
(wood)
Post-Pharaonic Period (ca. A.D. 395–700)
Faiyum
Length 27 cm; whorl diameter 4.8 cm
ACC. 2400-21

Child's? Bracelet
(ivory)
Post-Pharaonic Period (ca. A.D. 395–700)
Faiyum
Width 0.9 cm; diameter 4.8 cm
ACC. 2400-22

Pins
(bronze)
Roman Period (ca. 30 B.C.–A.D. 395)
el-Behnesa
Length 11–12.1 cm; head diameter 0.9–1 cm
ACC. 2400-25a
ACC. 2400-25b

Small Bowl
(calcite)
Dynasty III–IV (ca. 2750–2565 B.C.)
Sharona?
Height 3.8 cm; diameter 7.1 cm
ACC. 2400-28

Model Food Offerings
(ceramic)
Old Kingdom (ca. 2750–2250 B.C.)
Abydos
Length 3.4–6.7 cm; width 2–2.8 cm
ACC. 2400-31a
ACC. 2400-31d
ACC. 2400-31f

Mallet
(wood)
Dynasty XIX–XX (ca. 1295–1070 B.C.)
Deir el-Bahri
Height 26.3 cm; diameter 13.6 cm
ACC. 2940-8

Amulet Shaped like Human Ear
(glazed faience)
New Kingdom (ca. 1450–1070 B.C.)
Deir el-Bahri
Length 1.8 cm; width 1 cm
ACC. 2940-10b

Lentoid Beads
(faience)
Dynasty XVIII (ca. 1450–1295 B.C.)
Deir el-Bahri
Length 28 cm
ACC. 2940-11a

Mummy of Juvenile Cat
(animal remains, linen)
Late–Ptolemaic Periods (ca. 664–30 B.C.)
Length 29.3 cm; width 9 cm
ACC. 2983-6535

Cartonnage Fragment Depicting Nut
(cartonnage, paint)

Probably Ptolemaic Period (ca. 332–30 B.C.)
Length 14.2 cm; width 27 cm
ACC. 2983-6556

Top Half of Shabti
(faience)
Ptolemaic Period (ca. 332–30 B.C.)
Height 10.1 cm; width 3.5 cm
ACC. 2983-6563

Circular and Cylindrical Beads
(faience)
Late Period (ca. 664–332 B.C.)
Length 42 cm
ACC. 2983-6680

Necklace of Disk Beads
(faience)
New Kingdom (ca. 1539–1070 B.C.)?
Length 20.6 cm
ACC. 2983-6688

Necklace of Cylinder Beads and Amulet (later addition)
(faience)
New Kingdom (ca. 1539–1070 B.C.)?
Total length 144 cm
ACC. 2983-6691

Stela of Nesmontusenebtify
(limestone)
Dynasty XII (ca. 1979–1801 B.C.)
Height 64.2 cm; width 37.2 cm; thickness 8.2 cm
ACC. 2983-6702

Stamp Seal
(faience)
Late Period (ca. 664–332 B.C.)
Length 3.9 cm; width 2.2 cm; thickness 1 cm
ACC. 2983-6703

Funerary Cone of "King's Scribe" and "Overseer of the Double Granaries of Barley of Lower Egypt," Re
(ceramic, paint)
New Kingdom (ca. 1539–1070 B.C.)
Thebes?
Length 10.8 cm; diameter 7.5 cm
ACC. 2983-6708

Uraeus from Funerary Shrine
(gessoed wood, paint)
Late Period (ca. 664–332 B.C.)
Height 14.7 cm; width 3.8 cm
ACC. 2983-6709

Votive Statuette of Cat
(gessoed wood, paint)
Ptolemaic–Roman Periods (ca. 332 B.C.–A.D. 395)?
Height 16.8 cm; width 9.2 cm; depth 6.6 cm
ACC. 2983-6728

Amulet of Duamutef
(faience)
Late Period (ca. 664–332 B.C.)
Height 6.4 cm; width 1.8 cm
ACC. 2983-6735

Amulet of Imset
(faience)
Third Intermediate Period (ca. 1070–653 B.C.)

Height 7.4 cm; width 1.7 cm
ACC. 2983-6737

Amulet of Qebehsenef
(faience)
Third Intermediate Period
  (ca. 1070–653 B.C.)
Height 7.2 cm; width 1.2 cm
ACC. 2983-6738

Amulet of Hapy
(faience)
Late Period (ca. 664–332 B.C.)
Height 6.3 cm; width 1.5 cm
ACC. 2983-6739

Shabti *of Amenhotep*
(faience)
Third Intermediate Period
  (ca. 1070–653 B.C.)
Height 12.8 cm; width 3.8 cm
ACC. 2983-6758

Shabti *of Horsaast, Son of Hornakht*
(faience)
Late Period (ca. 664–332 B.C.)
Height 10.2 cm; width 2.6 cm
ACC. 2983-6760

Uninscribed Shabti
(limestone)
Dynasty XIX–XX (ca. 1295–
  1070 B.C.)
Height 17 cm; width 5.1 cm
ACC. 2983-6767

Uninscribed Overseer Shabti
(wood, paint)
Dynasty XIX–XX (ca. 1295–
  1070 B.C.)
Height 17 cm; width 5 cm
ACC. 2983-6771

Uninscribed Shabti
(wood, paint)
Dynasty XIX–XX (ca. 1295–
  1070 B.C.)
Height 21 cm; width 5 cm
ACC. 2983-6775

Statuette of Harpokrates
(bronze)
Ptolemaic Period (ca. 332–30 B.C.)
Height 11.5 cm; width 3.2 cm
ACC. 2983-6779

Perfume Bottle
(ceramic, paint)
Ptolemaic Period (ca. 332–30 B.C.)
Height 23.4 cm; diameter 3.4 cm
ACC. 2983-6846

Footed Bowl
(ceramic)
Roman Period or later (ca. 30 B.C.–
  A.D. 700)?
Height 8.4 cm; diameter 12 cm
ACC. 2983-6995

*Mummy Wrapping Inscribed with
  Chapter 125 for "Bearer," Horpen*
(linen, ink)
Late Period (ca. 664–332 B.C.)
Oxyrhynchus, 814?
Length 44.5 cm; width 10 cm
ACC. 3504-4

Inscribed Fragment of Cartonnage
(papyrus, plaster, paint, ink)
Ptolemaic Period (ca. 332–30 B.C.)
Hiba?, 114
Length 23.1 cm; width 17.5 cm
ACC. 3504-9

Cartonnage Mask for Mummy
(linen, plaster, paint)
Early Roman Period (ca. 30 B.C.–A.D.
  50)?
Height 30.5 cm; width 21 cm; depth
  18.7 cm
ACC. 3677-3a

Cartonnage Casing for Feet
(linen, plaster, paint)
Early Roman Period (ca. 30 B.C.–A.D.
  50)?
Height 26.5 cm; width 17 cm; depth
  20 cm
ACC. 3677-3b

Offering? Jar
(ceramic)
Dynasty III–IV (ca. 2750–2565 B.C.)
Mahasna, F111
Height 17 cm; diameter 9.5 cm
ACC. 4209-5

Rope and Hook
(date palm fiber, wood)
Ptolemaic Period (ca. 332–30 B.C.)?
Samhut
Hook: length 19.7 cm; width 8.8 cm
ACC. 4209-8

Bag-shaped Cosmetic Jar
(calcite)
Dynasty XII (ca. 1979–1801 B.C.)
Abydos, B13a
Height 5.2 cm; diameter 4.6 cm
ACC. 4210-5a

Lidded Kohl Pot
(anhydrite)
Dynasty XII (ca. 1979–1801 B.C.)
Abydos, B13a
Height 3.3 cm; diameter 3.4 cm
ACC. 4210-6

Leech-type Earring
(gold, paste)
Mid to late Dynasty XVIII (ca. 1450–
  1295 B.C.)
Abydos, T71
Length 1.2 cm; width 1.1 cm
ACC. 4210-8k3

Fly Amulets
(gold)
Mid to late Dynasty XVIII (ca. 1450–
  1295 B.C.)
Abydos, T71
Length 0.8 cm; width 0.4 cm
ACC. 4210-8m1 through 7

Wedjet-eye Amulets
(gold, paste)
Mid to late Dynasty XVIII (ca. 1450–
  1295 B.C.)
Abydos, T71
Length 0.7–0.8 cm; width 0.8 cm
ACC. 4210-8n1 through 6

Mirror with Its Handle Missing
(bronze)

Dynasty VI (ca. 2423–2250 B.C.)
Abydos, E242
Length 16.9 cm; width 15.5 cm
ACC. 4210-10

Stela of Wennefer
(limestone, paint)
Dynasty XXVI–early Dynasty XXVII
  (ca. 644–500 B.C.)
Abydos, South Cemetery? above R1
Height (incomplete) 24 cm; width
  26.8 cm; thickness 5.2 cm
ACC. 4210-13

Ibis Mummy in Coffin
(animal remains, linen, pottery)
Roman Period (ca. 30 B.C.–A.D. 300)
Abydos
Vessel: height 41.5 cm; diameter
  19 cm
ACC. 4918-4

Bread Mold
(ceramic)
Dynasty III–IV (ca. 2750–2565 B.C.)
Abydos, D126
Height 18.6 cm; diameter 23 cm
ACC. 4918-5

*Rectangular Beaded Collar for Mummy
  Shroud*
(faience)
Late Period (ca. 664–332 B.C.)
Length 50.4 cm; width 16.4 cm
ACC. 5511

Cobra's Head from Uraei Frieze
(diorite)
Late Dynasty XVIII (ca. 1347–
  1334 B.C.)
El Amarna, Maru-aten temple
Length 13 cm; width 15 cm
ACC. 7043-4

Statuette of Harpokrates
(bronze)
Ptolemaic Period (ca. 332–30 B.C.)
Height 15.1 cm; width 4.8 cm
ACC. 9007-30

Shabti *of "Fourth Prophet of
  Amun-Re," Nesamen*
(faience)
Third Intermediate Period
  (ca. 1070–653 B.C.)
Height 12.7 cm; width 4 cm
ACC. 9007-37

Shabti
(faience)
Third Intermediate Period
  (ca. 1070–653 B.C.)
Height 12.5 cm; width 4.9 cm
ACC. 9007-41

Head for Ibis Statuette or Mummy
(gilded bronze)
Late–Ptolemaic Periods (ca. 664–
  30 B.C.)
Height 6 cm; width 6.7 cm
ACC. 9007-44

Fragment of Biographical? Stela
(limestone)
Dynasty XIII–Second Intermediate
  Period (ca. 1801–1539 B.C.)

Height 37.7 cm; width 20.4 cm; thickness 7.6 cm
ACC. 9007-57

Unionid (Freshwater Mussel) Valve
(shell)
Neolithic–Predynastic Periods
  (ca. 5450–3100 B.C.)?
Length 11 cm; width 6.5 cm
ACC. 9074-2209a

Sickle Blade
(flint)
Neolithic–Predynastic Periods?
  (ca. 5450–3100 B.C.)
Length 4.8 cm; width 1.6 cm
ACC. 9074-2250

Face from Coffin
(wood, paint)
Third Intermediate Period (ca. 1070–
  653 B.C.)
Height 22.5 cm; width 14.2 cm
ACC. 9074-2252

Parts from Incense Burners
(bronze)
Ptolemaic Period (ca. 332–30 B.C.)?
Length 11 cm; width 5.8 cm
ACC. 9074-2260 (hand)
Height 5.5 cm; diameter 6.2 cm
ACC. 9074-2262 (cup)

Deep Bowl
(ceramic)
Lower Nubia, A Group (ca. 3200–
  2900 B.C.)
Height 17.8 cm; diameter 3.4 cm
ACC. 9074-2270b

Marl Ware Jar
(ceramic)
Dynasty I (ca. 3100–2900 B.C.)
Height 29.7 cm; diameter 9.3 cm
ACC. 9074-2300

High-shouldered Red Polished Ware Jar
(ceramic)
Naqada II (ca. 3650–3300 B.C.)
Height 18.6 cm; diameter 7.6 cm
ACC. 9074-2303

Red Polished Ware Jar
(ceramic)
Naqada II (ca. 3650–3300 B.C.)
Height 22.6 cm; diameter 8.7 cm
ACC. 9074-2308

Late Ware Bowl
(ceramic)
Late Naqada III–Dynasty I
  (ca. 3150–2900 B.C.)
Height 9.5 cm; diameter 21.7 cm
ACC. 9074-2312a

Rope
(fiber)
New Kingdom or later (ca. 1539 B.C.–
  A.D. 395)
Length 51.9 cm; diameter 1.5 cm
ACC. 9074-2406a

Lidded Basket
(rushes, palm leaves)
Probably New Kingdom (ca. 1539–
  1070 B.C.)

Height 6 cm; diameter 15 cm
ACC. 9074-2408a and b

Basket
(rushes, palm leaves)
New Kingdom (ca. 1539–1070 B.C.)
Height 11; diameter 34.5 cm
ACC. 9074-2410

Mummy of Nile Perch
(animal remains, linen, palm? fiber)
Late Period (ca. 664–332 B.C.)?
Length 20 cm; width 6.3 cm
ACC. 9074-2427g

Coffin? Fragment with Hieroglyphs Symbolizing Creation
(gessoed wood, paint)
Third Intermediate Period (ca. 1070–653 B.C.)
Length 21.2 cm; width 14.4 cm
ACC. 9074-2428

Coffin Fragment Depicting Deity
(gessoed wood, paint, bitumen)
New Kingdom (ca. 1539–1070 B.C.)
Length 44.2 cm; width 23 cm
ACC. 9074-2430

Pestle for Grinding Pigments
(basalt)
New Kingdom (ca. 1539–1070 B.C.)?
Length 3.8 cm; diameter 2.9 cm
ACC. 9074-2446

Model Servant of Striding Man
(wood, paint)
Dynasty XI–XII (ca. 2025–1801 B.C.)
Height 15; width 3.4 cm; depth 3.6 cm
ACC. 9074-2461

Pectoral Fragment Depicting Anubis
(wood)
New Kingdom (ca. 1539–1070 B.C.)
Length 7.2 cm; width 4.2 cm
ACC. 9074-2462

Model Ax
(bronze)
New Kingdom (ca. 1539–1070 B.C.)
Length 6.7 cm; width 3.6 cm
ACC. 9074-2470

Model Jar
(indurated limestone)
Late Old Kingdom–First Intermediate Period (ca. 2565–2025 B.C.)
Height 5.6 cm; diameter 3.8 cm
ACC. 9074-2479

Model Jar
(calcite)
Dynasty V–VI (ca. 2565–2250 B.C.)
Height 2.1 cm; diameter 2.2 cm
ACC. 9074-2483

Collared Vase
(calcite)
Dynasty VI–VIII (ca. 2423–2213 B.C.)
Height 17.9 cm; diameter 3.6 cm
ACC. 9074-2483a

Shouldered Bowl
(indurated limestone)

Old Kingdom (ca. 2750–2250 B.C.)
Height 3.5 cm; diameter 5.4 cm
ACC. 9074-2483c

Small Kohl Jar
(faience)
Dynasty XVIII (ca. 1539–1295 B.C.)
Height 5.8 cm; diameter 3.5 cm
ACC. 9074-2487

Small Jar
(faience)
Dynasty XVIII (ca. 1539–1295 B.C.)
Height 5.5 cm; diameter 4.4 cm
ACC. 9074-2488

Offering Tray
(ceramic)
First Intermediate Period–Dynasty XI (ca. 2250–1979 B.C.)
Length 29.5 cm; width 23.1 cm; thickness 3.5 cm
ACC. 9074-2497

Osiris Mold for Sprouting Grain
(ceramic)
Late Period (ca. 664–332 B.C.)
Length 27.2 cm; width 13.3 cm; thickness 5.6 cm
ACC. 9074-2499

Funerary Cone of "Overseer of the Treasury and All Contracts in Amun Temple" and "Scribe," Anen
(ceramic, paint)
Early Dynasty XVIII (ca. 1514–1479 B.C.)
Thebes, tomb 81?
Length 10.7 cm; diameter 10.6 cm
ACC. 9074-2507

Ostracon with Receipt of Amewenys's Taxes
(ceramic, ink)
Roman Period, in reign of Tiberius (A.D. 19–20)
Thebes
Length 9.1 cm; width 8.2 cm
ACC. 9074-2524

Ostracon with Hieroglyphic Inscription
(ceramic, paint)
New Kingdom (ca. 1539–1070 B.C.)?
Length 7 cm; width 6.6 cm
ACC. 9074-2534

Bag-shaped Jar
(ceramic)
Second Intermediate Period (ca. 1648–1539 B.C.)
Height 16.5 cm; diameter 8 cm
ACC. 9074-2551

Rough Ware Jar
(ceramic)
Naqada II (ca. 3650–3300 B.C.)
Height 16.5 cm; diameter 5.1 cm
ACC. 9074-2557

Globular Marl Ware Jar
(ceramic)
Dynasty I (ca. 3100–2900 B.C.)
Height 25.3 cm; diameter 12.1 cm
ACC. 9074-2559

Wavy-handled Ware Jar
(ceramic)

Naqada II (ca. 3650–3300 B.C.)
Height 26; diameter 11.5 cm
ACC. 9074-2560

Barbotine Ware Drinking Cup
(ceramic)
Mid Roman Period (ca. A.D. 100–200)
Height 7.1 cm; diameter 11.2 cm
ACC. 9074-2562a

Decorated Horn
(sheep/goat horn, paint)
Second Intermediate Period, Pan-grave (ca. 1648–1539 B.C.)
Length 30.8 cm; width 7 cm
ACC. 9074-2577

Decorated Horn
(sheep/goat horn, paint)
Second Intermediate Period, Pan-grave (ca. 1648–1539 B.C.)
Length 22 cm; width 8 cm
ACC. 9074-2597

Saw?
(flint)
Neolithic–Predynastic Periods (ca. 5450–3100 B.C.)
Length 5 cm; width 1.6 cm
ACC. 9074-2642

Projectile Point
(flint)
Neolithic, Faiyum A (ca. 5450–3850 B.C.)
Length 4.8 cm; width 2.3 cm
ACC. 9074-2652

Sickle Blade
(flint)
Neolithic–Predynastic Periods? (ca. 5450–3100 B.C.)
Length 5.9 cm; width 2.2 cm
ACC. 9074-2654

Awl
(bone)
Predynastic Period (ca. 4500–3100 B.C.)
Length 6.5 cm; width 1.9 cm
ACC. 9074-2660e

Projectile Point
(flint)
Neolithic, Faiyum A (ca. 5450–3850 B.C.)
Length 3.6 cm; width 2.5 cm
ACC. 9074-2662

Shallow Bowl
(indurated limestone)
Dynasty I (ca. 3100–2900 B.C.)
Height 3.8 cm; diameter 7.8 cm
ACC. 9074-2666

Pot Stand
(basketry)
New Kingdom (ca. 1539–1070 B.C.)
Diameter 15.5 cm; thickness 3 cm
ACC. 9074-2668

Brush
(grass or rushes)
New Kingdom (ca. 1539–1070 B.C.)?
Length 24.6 cm; width 10.2 cm
ACC. 9074-2669

Sokar Falcon
(gessoed wood, paint)
Late Period (ca. 664–332 B.C.)
Length 14.8 cm; width 4.9 cm; height 4.8 cm
ACC. 9074-2672

Mummy in Fetal Position
(human remains)
Predynastic Period (ca. 4500–3100 B.C.)?
Possibly Qift
Length 87 cm; width 48.5 cm; height 36.2 cm
ACC. 9074-99999

Ostracon of Receipt in Demotic
(limestone, ink)
Late Ptolemaic–early Roman Period (ca. 100 B.C.–A.D. 100)
Thebes?
Length 15.2 cm; width 13.4 cm
ACC. 9074-99999b

Shabti
(faience)
Third Intermediate Period (ca. 1070–653 B.C.)
Height 14.8 cm; width 4.9 cm
ACC. 11236-30

Unnamed Shabti
(faience)
Dynasty XXV (ca. 775–653 B.C.)
Height 11.9 cm; width 3.9 cm
ACC. 11983-6

Shabti of Wahibre, Son of Astirdis
(faience)
Late Period (ca. 664–332 B.C.)
Height 12.7 cm; width 3.2 cm
ACC. 11983-8

Head from Statuette of Amun-Re
(gilded basalt)
Late Period (ca. 664–332 B.C.)
Height 7.4 cm; width 3.7 cm; depth 2.6 cm
ACC. 11983-10

Scarab with Hieroglyphs
(glazed steatite)
Second Intermediate Period (ca. 1648–1539 B.C.)
Length 1.4 cm; width 0.9 cm
ACC. 11983-16b

Uninscribed Scarab
(steatite)
New Kingdom (ca. 1539–1070 B.C.)
Length 2.5 cm; width 1.8 cm
ACC. 11983-17

Scarab with Attachment Holes
(faience)
Third Intermediate Period (ca. 1070–653 B.C.)
Length 5.6 cm; width 3.9 cm
ACC. 11983-21

Ring with Tambourine-playing Bes-image
(faience)
Late Dynasty XVIII (ca. 1390–1295 B.C.)

Bezel: length 1.9 cm; width 1.1 cm;
 ring: diameter 2.2 cm
ACC. 11983-24

Model Fig
(faience)
Dynasty XVIII (ca. 1539–1295 B.C.)
Height 3 cm; width 2.4 cm
ACC. 11983-27

Rosette
(faience)
Dynasty XVIII (ca. 1539–1295 B.C.)
Diameter 1.6 cm; thickness 0.5 cm
ACC. 11983-28

Deep Bowl
(calcite)
Dynasty II (ca. 2900–2750 B.C.)
Saqqara?
Height 11.7 cm; diameter 14.4 cm
ACC. 13897

Linen Strip with Fringed End
(linen)
New Kingdom–Late Period
 (ca. 1539–332 B.C.)
Length 250 cm; width 14.5 cm
ACC. 17045-14a

Saucer-like Lamp
(ceramic)
New Kingdom (ca. 1539–1070 B.C.)?
Height 2.5 cm; diameter 6.9 cm
ACC. 19458-7

Lamp with Frog Design
(ceramic)
Mid to late Roman Period
 (ca. A.D. 150–300)
Length 6.8 cm; width 5 cm
ACC. 19458-33

High-shouldered Red Polished Ware Jar
(ceramic)
Late Naqada II (ca. 3500–3300 B.C.)
Hu
Height 29 cm; diameter 10.2 cm
ACC. 21537-20

Small Bag-shaped Jar
(ceramic)
First Intermediate Period (ca. 2250–
 2025 B.C.)
Hu?
Height 9.1 cm; diameter 6.4 cm
ACC. 21537-28

Late Ware Jar
(ceramic)
Late Naqada III (ca. 3150–3100 B.C.)
Hu?
Height 35.4 cm; diameter 12.9 cm
ACC. 21537-34

Late Ware Jar
(ceramic)
Naqada III (ca. 3300–3100 B.C.)
Hu?
Height 39.8 cm; diameter 11.6 cm
ACC. 21537-35

Large Rough Ware Jar with Pot Mark
(ceramic)
Naqada II (ca. 3650–3300 B.C.)

Hu
Height 38.8 cm; diameter 12.9 cm
ACC. 21537-37

Pot Stand
(ceramic)
New Kingdom (ca. 1539–1070 B.C.)
Hu
Height 5.2 cm; diameter 10.3 cm
ACC. 21537-45

Jar with Quatrefoil Mouth
(ceramic)
Dynasty XI–mid Dynasty XII
 (ca. 2025–1878 B.C.)
Hu?
Height 19.5 cm; diameter 9.1 cm
ACC. 21537-51

Blue Painted Ware Jar
(ceramic, paint)
Late Dynasty XVIII (ca. 1390–
 1295 B.C.)
Abydos, Umm el-Qa'ab
Height 21.5 cm; diameter 13 cm
ACC. 21537-52

Polished Jar with Long Neck
(ceramic)
Dynasty XVII–early Dynasty XVIII
 (ca. 1627/1606–1425 B.C.)
Hu, Y51
Height 19.3 cm; diameter 7.1 cm
ACC. 21537-53

Polychrome Jar with Undulating Neck
(ceramic, paint)
Dynasty XIX–XX (ca. 1295–
 1070 B.C.)
Abydos or Hu
Height 14.6 cm; diameter 4.7 cm
ACC. 21537-57

Lid to Incised Ware Bowl
(ceramic, paste)
Late Naqada I (ca. 3750–3650 B.C.)
Hu?
Height 5.7 cm; diameter 9 cm
ACC. 21537-64

Ptah-Sokar Amulet
(faience)
Third Intermediate Period (ca. 1070–
 653 B.C.)?
Hu?
Length 3.5 cm; width 1.4 cm
ACC. 21537-86

Base of Nonfunctional Canopic Jar
(limestone)
Third Intermediate Period
 (ca. 1070–653 B.C.)
Hu?
Height 20.1 cm; diameter 10 cm
ACC. 21537-91

Canopic Jar Lid of Qebehsenef
(calcite)
Late Period (ca. 664–332 B.C.)?
Hu?
Height 10.2 cm; diameter 12.6 cm
ACC. 21537-95

Canopic Jar Lid of Hapy
(calcite)
Late Period (ca. 664–332 B.C.)?
Abydos?
Height 15.3 cm; diameter 11.2 cm
ACC. 21537-97

Fragment from Sekhmet Statue
(granite)
Mid Dynasty XVIII, reign of Amen-
hotep III (ca. 1390–1352 B.C.)
Deir el-Bahri?
Length 21 cm; width 15 cm; thick-
ness 5 cm
ACC. 21537-100

Uninscribed Shabti
(metamorphic rock)
Dynasty XXV (ca. 775–653 B.C.)
Abydos or Hu
Height 11.3 cm; width 6.2 cm
ACC. 21537-102

Carinated Jar
(ceramic)
Dynasty IV–VI (ca. 2675–2250 B.C.)
Hu, W95
Height 13 cm; diameter 9.5 cm
ACC. 21537-119

Headrest
(wood)
New Kingdom (ca. 1539–1070 B.C.)
Length 21.5; width 7.7 cm; height
 20.5 cm
ACC. 21538-14

Model Servant of Woman Grinding?
(wood, paint)
Dynasty XI–XII (ca. 2025–
 1801 B.C.)
Height 15.6 cm; width 4 cm
ACC. 21538-16

Model Servant of Seated Man
(wood, paint)
Dynasty XI–XII (ca. 2025–
 1801 B.C.)
Height 15.1 cm; width 3.8 cm
ACC. 21538-17

Foot Belonging to Falcon Statue
(bronze)
Late–Ptolemaic Periods (ca. 664–
 30 B.C.)
Height 9.3 cm; width 2.2 cm; depth
 8.9 cm
ACC. 21538-18

Cylinder Vase
(limestone)
Dynasty III–IV (ca. 2750–2565 B.C.)
Height 17.1 cm; diameter 16.3 cm
ACC. 21538-23

Inscribed Canopic Jar Base
(calcite)
Late Period (ca. 664–332 B.C.)?
Height 22.5 cm; diameter 12 cm
ACC. 21538-26

Fragment with Nebmaatre's Cartouche
(diabase)
Mid Dynasty XVIII (ca. 1390–
 1352 B.C.)

Length 18.5 cm; width 15 cm; thickness 4.7 cm
ACC. 21538-32

Fragment with Uraeus on Crown
(limestone, paint)
Early Dynasty XVIII, reign of Amenhotep I (ca. 1514–1493 B.C.)?
Length 9.5 cm; width 14 cm; thickness 2.8 cm
ACC. 21538-37

Shouldered Jar
(indurated limestone)
Dynasty I (ca. 3100–2900 B.C.)
Abydos?
Height 5.5 cm; diameter 6.9 cm
ACC. 21539-10

*Statuette of Ahmose, Dedicated by His
 Brother, Wadjshemesisew*
(limestone, paint)
Dynasty XVIII (ca. 1539–1295 B.C.)
Deir el-Bahri?
Height 17 cm; width 8.4 cm; depth
 19 cm
ACC. 21539-14

Mummy of Paheter
(human remains, linen, cartonnage)
Early Roman Period, reign of
Augustus? (ca. 30 B.C.–A.D. 14)
Hawara?
Length 160 cm; width 43 cm; depth
 29 cm
ACC. 22266-1a

Relief Fragment
(limestone, paste)
Dynasty XII–XIII (ca. 1979–1627/
 1606 B.C.)
Length 14.3 cm; width 17 cm; thickness 4.4 cm
ACC. 29691-218

Stela Dedicated to Sobek-Re
(limestone, paint)
New Kingdom (ca. 1539–1070 B.C.)
Height (incomplete) 17.2 cm; width
 19 cm; thickness 2.9 cm
ACC. 29691-219

Coin with Head of Ptolemaic Ruler?
(bronze)
Ptolemaic Period (ca. 332–30 B.C.)
Diameter 3.1 cm; thickness 0.5 cm
ACC. 33444-23

Wedjet-eye Amulet
(faience)
New Kingdom–Late Period
 (ca. 1539–332 B.C.)
Length 3.5 cm; width 2.5 cm
ACC. 34096-1a

APPENDIX 2

Previous Publication of Objects in The Walton Hall of Ancient Egypt

The following bibliography makes no claim to completeness; it is designed to acquaint interested individuals with original publication sources of the Egypt Exploration Society material and any other subsequent publication with significant treatment of Carnegie objects.

Allen, Hamilton Ford. "Two Mummy-labels in the Carnegie Museum." *Annals of the Carnegie Museum* VIII, no. 2 (1912): 218–21. Accessions 1948-10 and 4614.

Bedell, Ellen Dailey. "The Kem Funerary Stela." *Carnegie Magazine* XLIX, no. 5 (1975): 206–16. Accession 21538-38.

Grenfell, B.P., A.S. Hunt, and D.G. Hogarth. *Fayûm Towns and Their Papyri*. Vol. III, *Memoir of the Graeco-Roman Branch* (London, 1901). Accession 1948.

Haldane, Cheryl Ward. "A Fourth Dahshur Boat." *Journal of Egyptian Archaeology* LXXI (1985): 174. Accession 1842-1.

Hunt, A.S. *The Oxyrhynchus Papyri, Part III*. Vol. V, *Memoir of the Graeco-Roman Branch* (London,1903). Accessions 3504-1, 3504-5, 3504-6, and 3504-7.

———. *The Oxyrhynchus Papyri, Part IV*. Vol. VI, *Memoir of the Graeco-Roman Branch* (London, 1904). Accessions 3504-2, 3504-3, and 3504-4.

Naville, Edouard. *The Temple of Deir El Bahari, Part III*. Vol. XXVI, *Memoir of The Egypt Exploration Fund* (London, 1898). Accession 2940.

———. *The Temple of Deir El Bahari, Part IV*. Vol. XXIX, *Memoir of The Egypt Exploration Fund* (London, 1901). Accession 3079.

Owsley, David T. "New Ancient Egyptian Art." *Carnegie Magazine* XLVII, no. 6 (1973): 226–30. Accession 4558-2.

Peet, T.E. *The Cemeteries of Abydos, Part II 1911–1912*. Vol. XXXIV, *Memoir of The Egypt Exploration Society* (London, 1914). Accessions 4210, 4558, and 4698.

Peet, T.E., and W.L.S. Loat. *The Cemeteries of Abydos, Part III 1912–1913*. Vol. XXXV, *Memoir of The Egypt Exploration Society* (London, 1913). Accessions 4918 and 4919.

Petrie, Sir W.M. Flinders. *Abydos, Part I 1902*. Vol. XXII, *Memoir of The Egypt Exploration Fund* (London, 1902). Accession 2231.

———. *Abydos, Part II 1903*. Vol. XXIV, *Memoir of The Egypt Exploration Fund* (London, 1903). Accession 2231.

———. *Diospolis Parva*. Vol. XX, *Special Extra Publication of The Egypt Exploration Fund* (London, 1901). Accessions 1234 and 1168.

———. *Memphis, Part I*. Vol. XV, *The British School of Archaeology in Egypt* (London, 1909). Accession 3755.

———. *The Palace of Apries (Memphis II)*. Vol. XVII, *The British School of Archaeology in Egypt* (London, 1909). Accession 3755.

———. *The Royal Tombs of the Earliest Dynasties 1900, Part I*. Vol. XVIII, *Memoir of The Egypt Exploration Fund* (London, 1900). Accession 1917.

———. *The Royal Tombs of the Earliest Dynasties 1901, Part II*. Vol. XXI, *Memoir of The Egypt Exploration Fund* (London, 1901). Accessions 1662 and 1917.

Randall-MacIver, David, and A.C. Mace. *El-Amrah and Abydos, 1899–1901*. Vol. XXIII, *Special Extra Publication of The Egypt Exploration Fund* (London, 1902). Accession 1917.

Woolley, C. Leonard. "Excavations at Tell El-Amarna." *Journal of Egyptian Archaeology* VIII (1922): 48–82. Accession 7043 and probably Accession 7106.

APPENDIX 3

Chronology of Ancient Egypt

Neolithic Period, ca. 5450–3850 B.C.

Predynastic Period, ca. 4500–3100 B.C.

Badarian, ca. 4500–3800 B.C.
Naqada I, ca. 3850–3650 B.C.
Naqada II, ca. 3650–3300 B.C.
Naqada III, ca. 3300–3100 B.C.

Early Dynastic Period, ca. 3100–2750 B.C.

Dynasty I, ca. 3100–2900 B.C.
Dynasty II, ca. 2900–2750 B.C.

Old Kingdom, ca. 2750–2250 B.C.

Dynasty III, ca. 2750–2675 B.C.
Dynasty IV, ca. 2675–2565 B.C.
Dynasty V, ca. 2565–2423 B.C.
Dynasty VI, ca. 2423–2250 B.C.

First Intermediate Period, ca. 2250–2025 B.C.

Dynasty VIII, ca. 2250–2213 B.C.
Dynasty IX–X, ca. 2213–2025 B.C.
Dynasty XI, ca. 2122–2025 B.C.

Middle Kingdom, ca. 2025–1627/1606 B.C.

Dynasty XI, ca. 2025–1979 B.C.
Dynasty XII, ca. 1979–1801 B.C.
Dynasty XIII, ca. 1801–1627/1606 B.C.

Second Intermediate Period, ca. 1648–1539 B.C.

Dynasty XV, ca. 1648–1540 B.C.
Dynasty XVII, ca. 1627/1606–1539 B.C.

New Kingdom, ca. 1539–1070 B.C.

Dynasty XVIII, ca. 1539–1295 B.C.
Dynasty XIX, ca. 1295–1185 B.C.
Dynasty XX, ca. 1185–1070 B.C.

Third Intermediate Period, ca. 1070–653 B.C.

Dynasty XXI, ca. 1070–945 B.C.
Dynasty XXII, ca. 945–718 B.C.
Dynasty XXIII, ca. 820–718 B.C.
Dynasty XXIV, ca. 730–712 B.C.
Dynasty XXV, ca. 775–653 B.C.

Late Period, ca. 664–332 B.C.

Dynasty XXVI, ca. 664–525 B.C.
Dynasty XXVII, ca. 525–404/401 B.C.
Dynasty XXIX, ca. 399–380 B.C.
Dynasty XXX, ca. 380–342 B.C.
Dynasty XXXI, ca. 342–332 B.C.

Ptolemaic Period, ca. 332–30 B.C.

Macedonian Dynasty, ca. 332–305 B.C.
Ptolemaic Dynasty, ca. 310/305–30 B.C.

Roman Period, 30 B.C.–A.D. 395

Note: Egyptologists today cannot find any evidence to
support the existence of Dynasty VII but, in order
to avoid confusion, have not revised the dynastic system.
Dynasty XIV, XVI, and XXVIII were composed of
minor rulers and are not listed in this chronology.

INDEX AND GLOSSARY